Jesus Alone
The Quest for the Living Oracle

Clayton Todd Kirk

ST. LOUIS, MISSOURI

Copyright © 2012 by Clayton Todd Kirk.
All rights reserved. No part of this book may be reproduced or transmitted in any form or by any means, electronic or mechanical, including photocopying, recording, or by any information storage and retrieval system, without permission in writing from the copyright owner. For permission or to reuse content, please contact librarydad68@yahoo.com

All quotes in this paper are from public domain sources including scripture quotations from Alexander Campbell's "Living Oracles" translation of the New Testament (1832).

Paperback: 978-1-60350-021-0

Published by Lucas Park Books
www.lucasparkbooks.com

Printed in the United States of America

Dedication

To my mother who taught me to seek the Spirit in all things, and to my father who taught me to test all things.

Contents

Foreword: Apology for a Title. 1
Chapter 1: Introduction. 3
Chapter 2: The Body. 14
    Introduction
    Jesus and John
    Facing Doubts
    First Sermon
    Fishing for People
    Spreading the Word
    Resisting Evil
    Eating with Sinners
    Lord of the Sabbath
    Good Things
    Growth
    Kingdom of God
    Wisdom's Children
    Elijah Reborn
    Fruit
    Do Unto Others
    Riches
    Your Neighbor
    Seeking
    Approaching Jerusalem
    Remember what God has Wrought
    The Passion

Chapter 3: Conclusions. 47
Appendix I: What Happened to Jesus' Body? 53
Appendix II:
    What Paul Says the Church "Always" Believed. 56
Appendix III:
    Early Divisions within Christianity. 58
Appendix IV:
    Contradictions and Errors in the Gospels?. 60
Bibliography 65

Foreword

Apology for a Title

> "We set out determined to sacrifice everything to truth, and follow her, wherever she might lead the way."
> — Alexander Campbell

The year 1825 stands in historical memory as the year that Alexander Campbell made his final and irrevocable break from the Redstone Baptist Association and set out to found a truly new American religious movement. From this moment on, the Restoration Movement would be something distinct, and would eventually give rise to the modern Church of Christ, Christian Church, and Disciples of Christ.

What is far less well known, but equally important in the eyes of the current author, is the contribution that Alexander Campbell made to the field of bible translation in the very same year. More than a century before the N.I.V. was even an idea, Campbell began a very similar and high quality translation of the entire New Testament in modern English. Campbell's translation was both to be the first modern-language translation as well as the first translation to use the now standard "critical" Greek text instead of the "Textus Receptus" of the K.J.V. Although it became fairly popular among Restorationist believers in the 1840's and 1850's, it is now all but forgotten. By all rights the Campbell bible project may be the most under-rated and under-appreciated contribution to biblical study and scholarship in the modern era.[1]

The Campbell translation came to be known as "The Living Oracles" and was completed in its final rescension in 1832 – the same year that the three separate Restoration groups from across the U.S. met and shook hands in Lexington, KY to form a unified movement. Thus the year marks the beginning of both the unified Restoration Movement (Disciples of Christ) and the first modern New Testament bible.

The present author has commandeered the title of Campbell's work as an "ebenezer" of sorts, to the brilliance and foresight of Alexander Campbell and his desire to get at the root of all things spiritual. This book is quite literally "A Quest for the Living Oracle."

Throughout this book, Campbell's "Living Oracles" is quoted as the translation of choice for two principle reasons. The first, as mentioned previously, is a celebration, or perhaps even a memorial to Campbell's great accomplishment. The second is a more practical reason: I can use as much of Campbell's New Testament as I need without seeking copyright permission, as any copyright has long expired. I also must confess I like the idea of using a translation free of the encumbrances of Mammon.

There is a true separation of the Church and the dollar here: anyone can obtain and read Campbell's bible for free and anyone can quote from it without permission. The fiercely independent Alexander Campbell smiles from his perch in Glory.

If desired, the reader is encouraged to compare with his or her own favorite translation. But in the mean they will find that Campbell's follows the N.I.V. quite closely.

---

[1] The eminent biblical scholar, Edgar Goodpeed (1871–1962) gave Campbell's translation the following complement: "Campbell's translation was the first of the modern versions. Far from writing his pet doctrines into the Bible, Campbell...cleared away confusion and corrected many inaccuracies of the hallowed King James..."

Chapter 1

Introduction

"On Christ the solid rock I stand, all other ground is sinking sand." – Edward Mote (Hymn)

This book is written, first and foremost, to people who have a passion for knowing Jesus. Not necessarily a passion for religion or even for the organized church, but a passion to know Him: A passion so great that they might be willing even to reconsider cherished cultural and religious assumptions. A person who might be willing to tread the same rocky path tread by the forefathers of the Restoration Movement – Men who by-and-large preferred the Truth to fame or earthly notoriety, as evidenced by their virtual anonymity even within the movements they founded.

The Church of Christ, in particular, is famous for their assertion that they "do not believe" in creeds. Certainly in a relative sense this is an accurate statement. The Restoration Movement (and particularly the Church of Christ) is very likely the least overtly creedal movement in all of Christendom. Often on a given Sunday morning, one can hear a Church of Christ preacher preach "the bible only."

However, this author suggests that nevertheless there are assumptions guiding the doctrinal formulations and theology of the Restoration Movement – *defacto* creeds, if you will. Some of these might be considered "common sense" within the movement as culturally formed norms often are. For example, it is assumed that all four gospels harmonize well, describe basically the same events, and are theologically similar. It is further assumed that the entire message of the New Testament is consistent and that Paul accurately reflects the intent of Jesus and the early Christians. Is it assumed that the New Testament, and especially the Gospels, contain no historical or biographical inaccuracies, or at least that that any inaccuracies that might exist are theologically and doctrinally insignificant – Common Sense, no doubt, in many Christian denominations and movements.

The author remembers hearing a preacher proclaim from the pulpit that "anything worth believing is worth testing." If these assumptions are indeed true than they should easily pass scrutiny. If they are not, then perhaps they should be reformulated or reconsidered. It seems reasonable to assume that The Word-of-God should at least pass the tests to which we regularly submit our scientific, social, political, and economic ideas in our modern world.

The idea of the common witness of the four gospels and Paul to the person, deeds, and message of Jesus is among the most deeply embedded of these creeds in the collective psychology of Restorationist believers. The principle question the author would like to propose is thus: Do each of the four gospels in fact portray the same "Jesus"? In other words, are they compatible? Is there any evidence that they are NOT compatible?

Mark vs. John

Mark is almost universally considered to be the first gospel written. Some scholars date it perhaps as early as 50 A.D. while very few would suggest a date later than 70 A.D. Most of the data in Mark is also found in Matthew and Luke, as they used Mark as a resource. Matthew and Luke were written about 20 years after Mark, and the Gospel of John at least 10 years after that. Mark is also the gospel almost universally considered by scholars – liberal, conservative, Restorationist, and otherwise — as the one most likely to have been written by someone with a direct historical connection to Jesus; most likely "John Mark," a follower of the Apostle Peter (*cf* I Peter 5:13).[1] If we isolate Mark's theology for consideration, apart from the other witnesses and mainstream Christian tradition, there are some striking "oddities."

The most glaring theological omission in Mark is the total absence of Atonement Theology. Nowhere in Mark does Jesus unambiguously claim to be an ultimate sacrifice for the sins of the world. In fact, he is frequently seen as deflecting any attempts at deification by his audience (*cf* Mark 10:18). Often a discourse or healing will end with the words, "your Faith has made you whole," often followed by a "go and sin no more." The focus is primarily on convincing a person to honestly clarify their intentions and take responsibility for their relationship with God (*cf* Mark 4:23–25). How very different from the Gospel of John, for example, where Jesus declares his unique divinity, as well as his role as an offering for the sins of humankind, in no less than five unambiguous passages (*cf* John 8:58).

Another oddity of Mark, relative to mainstream Christian tradition, is the paucity of claims to unique divinity. Nowhere in Mark does Jesus claim to be the only Son of God as he so often does in the book of John. He is referred to as "Holy" and even as "son of God," but never as the unique and only Son of God (traditionally "only begotten") as in the Gospel of John. In fact, Jesus himself goes to great lengths to identify himself as the "Son of Man," (from the Aramaic "Barnasha;")[2] a somewhat ambiguous term which may even mean something as simple as "mortal man" in English. In any event it was not a commonly used term within Jewish culture of the time; the only clear defining reference[3] to the term being from the book of Daniel (7:13) where it is equally ambiguous as to meaning. However, it is unclear from the text in Daniel what term was to connote.

---

1 In 130 A.D. the Bishop Papias writes that he had heard from "The Presbyter" that Mark was based on the remembrances of the Apostle Peter as recalled by Mark (probably John Mark). If Papias' statement is accurate then this assertion takes us back to biblical times.

2 "ben adam" in O.T. Hebrew.

3 The term itself is mentioned many times in Ezekiel and Daniel but is not defined clearly

In any event, the Son of Man in Daniel was "given" authority and was not God himself. Also Jesus may have used the term independently of the witness and context of the book of Daniel.

In the few Markian passages where we get a hint or reference that might be interpreted as evidence for unique divinity, Jesus himself almost always cautions the person making the claim (*cf* Mark 3:12). He is frequently reported as giving a stern warning not to reveal (or perhaps "repeat") the claim of divinity. Take for example the puzzling assertion from Mark 10:17 –

> *As he went out into the road, one came running to him, who, kneeling, asked him, Good Teacher, what must I do to inherit eternal life? Jesus answered, Why do you call me good? God alone is good.*

Another peculiarity of Mark is the focus it takes on the life of Jesus. The book of John is all about Jesus-the-Divine-Person. It is from John that we get the references to "Bread of Life," "I am the Door," as well as unambiguous references to Jesus' sinlessness and unique divinity. However, the story in Mark is very different in focus. In Mark it is predominantly about what Jesus says and does rather than who he is as a divine being. Although there are references to Jesus' divinity in Mark, they are more along the line of punctuations and "flavorings." The bulk of the book is about Jesus' deeds – the natural implication being that we should strive to be like Jesus, rather than worship Jesus as a God (as in John).

In addition Mark (as it was originally written) has no birth or post-resurrection accounts of Jesus – despite the fact that it was possibly compiled by a follower of Peter. The narrative (according to most scholars) originally ended at vs. 16:8 with the women in shock and not knowing what to do next:

> *The women then getting out, fled from the tomb, seized with trembling and consternation; but said nothing to any one, they were so terrified.*

In most bibles, including the NIV, there is a footnote identifying this as the original ending of the gospel. Although omission doesn't necessarily prove irrelevance (or ignorance), the omission taken in balance with the other peculiarities of Mark begs a question: If Mark were preserving the core of Jesus' life for future generations wouldn't he at least include his virgin birth and post-resurrection? It's a bit hard to imagine that those distinctives wouldn't pass the final edit. In our modern Christian culture those two distinctives (Jesus' miraculous birth and rising) are usually the first things mentioned in a conversation between a devout Christian and a potential convert.

A Ransom for Many

There is only one seemingly unambiguous reference to something like "atonement" in the book of Mark. Many bible students can quote it from memory: "...the Son of Man came not to be served, but to serve, and to give his life as a ransom for many" (Mark 10:45).

As mentioned previously, the fact that this concept is only mentioned once in the entire gospel is itself reason to be skeptical of the "atonement" interpretation. However, the present author feels that there is another logical and valid reason to doubt the atonement interpretation of the word "ransom."

The word "ransom," is usually defended by conservative scholars etymologically. The actual Greek word is "Lutron," and does literally mean something very much like the English "ransom." It is related to the Greek "Luo," which connotes the sense of "loosing" or perhaps "setting free."

However, literal meanings and cultural meanings are not always in concert. The more important question is what the word meant in the culture of 1st Century Palestine among Greek-speaking Jews. It is fairly clear from history that the word "Lutron" did not necessarily connote the modern meaning of "atonement" (or perhaps even "ransom") in its colloquial and contextually appropriate use.

An almost identical use of the phrase "gave his life as a ransom (Lutron) for many" can be found in the Greek book of 4th Maccabees, Chapter 17, which was written during Jesus' lifetime by people culturally similar to those who compiled our New Testament. It is a book that appears in many ancient Christian bibles, but has never been part of the mainstream Catholic or Protestant canonical scriptures.

The chapter is a sermon based on events recorded in the apocryphal book of 2 Maccabees,[4] Chapter 7 – itself an important passage as it contains one of the first unambiguous historical references to the afterlife in the Jewish culture. In the story, the pagan ruler Antiochus commands a family of eight persons (seven grown children and their aged mother) to eat pork in violation of Jewish law. The mother is made to watch as each of her seven sons is subjected to gory tortures that would elicit a cringe from Hannibal Lecter. I will not recount them here, but they are decidedly "Rated 'R'."

Each son stands nobly praying to God, as they take their last breaths and are murdered in turn. And then as the guards finally reach for the mother, she throws herself into the flames rather than be defiled by Antiochus' minions.

Recounting the story, the author of 4th Maccabees remarks, "they became a ransom (Lutron) for the sins of our nation… through their blood, an expiation for the preservation of Israel …their sacrifice being an example to our own endurance" (Ch. 17, vs. 21–23).

Here we have a direct, culturally-contextually relevant use of the term "Lutron" from Jesus' time, the meaning of which is clearly nothing like our modern concept of "atonement" taught in many churches.

The term "ransom," as used here, seems to mean something much more like "noble example" or perhaps "symbolic example." The mother was a "ransom" because she did not compromise her faith and in so doing, became a symbol for other Jews to remember and emulate. I think this is exactly how the term should be applied to Jesus in Mark 10:45, and in the context, where Jesus has been speaking of self-sacrifice, it makes perfect sense.

To summarize; the oldest, most reliable biography of Jesus from the New Testament has no clear references to the Atonement, no miraculous birth accounts, no physical resurrection from the dead, and is quite dissimilar from the much-later-written Gospel of John.

So, what would Christianity be like if all we had was the Gospel of Mark? We would have a captivating story about an

---

[4] This is a considered a canonical book of the bible by Catholics and Orthodox churches and appears in their bibles, as well as in "common bibles."

amazing Jewish man, blessed and chosen by God, who spent his life showing compassion and urging others to seek the Kingdom-of-God in their hearts. A man who was so dedicated to his cause and convictions that he would not surrender them. He chose death instead.

The Riddle of Paul

Those who have grown up in the Church are accustomed to reading Paul into the Gospels. It is generally assumed that Paul's faith and practice were more-or-less identical to that described in Mark and the synoptics. However, upon close inspection and comparison there are some interesting "oddities" in Paul as there are in Mark. Above, it was suggested what Christianity might look like today if all we had were the book of Mark. But what would Christianity look like if all we had were the books of Paul and those immediately based on the interpretations of Paul (such as the book of Hebrews)?

Since Paul emphasized the Atonement and Faith in the risen Christ over all else, we would have a Christianity that actually looks a lot more like the Christianity we actually do have. Our current expressions of Christianity look a lot more like what one might naturally derive from the letters of Paul than they do the words (and theology) of Jesus recorded in Matthew, Mark, and Luke.

Paul's theology is 100% about the risen Christ. Nowhere in his letters does Paul ever describe a single deed of Jesus. Paul's chief concern and source for doctrine seems to be mystical and transcendental rather than concrete and historical. In the book of Mark described earlier, there is an almost obsessive concern with what Jesus said and did – in Paul's letters neither of these is to be found. It is from Paul's writings that the Protestant maxim "Salvation by Faith Alone" was derived.[5] It could not have been so derived from the synoptic gospels. Paul is primarily concerned with the Atonement, while the Jesus of Mark can be more accurately described as "Karmic."[6]

---

[5] James may have also had a problem with Paul's theology – *cf* James 2:17-23

[6] Karma is the cosmic principle of cause and effect - the idea that all actions, whether good or evil, must run their course. All actions done to others must also be experienced by the doer. Thus the only way to improve one's situation is to modify the way one acts and the choices one makes.

Perhaps the most shocking "omission" of Paul when examined objectively is his absolute silence on the issue of the "Empty Tomb." In his letters, Paul takes on many issues that a typical Christian might consider far less important than the resurrection – thus Paul was not beyond addressing a range of theological and moral speculations. But on this central issue of what happened to Christ after his death, Paul is silent about the details. The closest he comes to describing that part of the faith is in I Corinthians 15. In this context it is fairly clear that Paul understands Jesus to have had what we moderns would probably describe as a "mystical" or "spiritual" resurrection.[7] Only a few verses away from his statement "also [Jesus] was seen by me," Paul spends the rest of Chapter 15 arguing for a spiritual and against a physical resurrection.[8] In fact Paul specifically states that mortal bodies and resurrection bodies are qualitatively different:

> *Just so is the resurrection of the dead. It is sown in corruption – it is raised in incorruption: it is sown in dishonor – it is raised in glory: it is sown in weakness – it is raised in power: it is sown an animal body – it is raised a spiritual body" (I Corinthians 15:42–44).*

A few lines earlier, Paul tells us that Jesus appeared to the apostles in the same manner that He appeared to Paul. From other accounts[9] we know that this was a spiritual appearance and not a physical one. It would have been very simple (and seemingly important) at this point for Paul to have stated "but Jesus was actually present in a physical body and walked out of his tomb," but such a qualifier is nowhere to be found – in this, or in any other of Paul's writings (*cf* I Corinthians 15:7–9). The conclusion is uncomfortable, but inescapable: Either Paul didn't think the Empty Tomb was important, or, he wasn't aware of it. This also explains Paul's emphasis on the Risen (mystical) Christ – the Risen Christ was the same Christ (both in quality and appearance) as the one that survived the resurrection.

---

7 also *cf* Ephesians 4:10

8 "But some one will say, How can the dead be raised up? and with what kind of body do they come? Simpleton!" – I Cor. 15:35

9 *cf* Acts 9

So we are faced with a decision about how to reconcile these differences among the New Testament writings. The solutions tend to fall into two camps. The first is by far the most popular – simply amalgamate the accounts of the New Testament and ignore any differences as "minor." The second would be to give primacy to either Paul (including John which is assumed to be based on Pauline ideas) or Jesus (of the synoptics). The default position for number two is usually to squeeze Jesus into Paul's mould rather than the other way around. This is mostly due to the historical emphasis of the organized church on the works and words of Paul which have indirectly influenced even the most primitive and reconstructive of the protestant movements – such as the Cambelite movement. I would like to suggest however, that there is a Third Way which is fully compatible with the spirit of the Reformation in general and the Restorationist Movement in particular.

The present author would like to make a bold suggestion: To clear up the aforementioned inconsistencies and apparent contradictions in the text,[10] we should shift from a fundamentalist "bible only" strategy to a Christ-centric "Jesus-only" strategy. To do this we would need to construct a source document which pulls together the most likely words and deeds of Jesus, and then use said document as a basis upon which to build our faith. Just as our Restoration forefathers shifted from "church tradition" to "bible alone" because of the weight of evidence, we should now, based on the weight of 200-years of evidence compiled since the dawn of the Restoration, shift to a "Jesus-only" lodestar. What is being suggested here is that we apply what we know from textual studies and scientific methodology to embark on a sort-of "Christological Criticism" to construct a source document that most closely resembles the original words and deeds of Jesus.

There are essentially four categories of tools at our disposal for such a project: 1) New Testament criticism, 2) Textual discoveries that shed light on the original text, 3) Extra biblical sources, and 4) Comparative religion. Among other benefits, principle in the field of NT Criticism is the ability to determine

---

[10] see Appendix 4 for an expanded list of major contradiction and errors in the canonical Gospel texts

which of duplicate readings is the oldest and most likely original. Textual discoveries such as the Dead Sea Scrolls contribute to this process as well and also aid in the reconstruction of cultural norms for the time period of interest. There are also a few precious extra-biblical sources for Jesus' words that take us back to a time before Mark was written, but not many. Included in this group may be some phrases from the Gospel of Thomas as well as some fragments and secondary quotes from letters. These discoveries all provide cultural insights and information on the nuances of culture, philology, and idiom. Comparative religion has been the least used of the aforementioned tools for building the source document. Comparative religion searches for patterns that are common to the religious context of interest. For our current purposes that context includes the cultural East and Near-East.

Thus, the overriding purpose of this project is the following: To come as close as possible to the spirit of what Jesus actually said, and to build a useable source document ("gospel") from the conclusions. In short, to recapture the actual religion of Jesus of Nazareth divorced from the accretions of history, and based upon what he actually said and meant.

Several authors and scholars have taken on parts of this task. The bibliography provides a summary of the major works in this field, all of which were carefully read, studied and compared by the present author. Among these, two in particular became the guiding documents for this project (with close reference and comparison to the other documents mentioned in the bibliography): *The Gospel of Jesus* (Funk, 1999) and *A Life of Jesus* (Goodspeed, 1956). These became valuable sources of information, although neither was quoted from directly. Both of these books represent a conservative assessment, in the judgment of scholars, as to what Jesus actually said. *The Gospel of Jesus* is particularly useful towards this end in that it represents the conclusions of 150 researchers dedicated to re-discovering what Jesus said divorced from later accretions of history and prior to the onslaught of organized Christian theology. Edgar Goodspeed, author of *A Life of Jesus,* is one of the greatest

---

11 Campbell was the first to translate the NT into modern English, Goodspeed the first to translate the entire Bible.

American biblical scholars of the 20th century, and the first translator of the entire bible into colloquial English.[11]

By comparison with these and other sources, the present author arrived at a conservative consensus of Jesus' sayings to be rendered in modern English. Most of these sayings come from the book of Mark, but a few are derived from the other canonical Gospels as well as a few extra-biblical ancient sources such as *The Gospel of Thomas*[12] and the *Oxyrhynchus* fragments.[13]

Following the suggested source document described above is a chapter outlining the conclusions of the project which will attempt to address the following questions: Who was Jesus? What did he say about himself? And how much did the real Jesus differ from the Christ-of-Faith?

---

12 Discovered in the 1940's – thought to be roughly contemporaneous with the Gospel of John

13 The general consensus is that extra-biblical sources have added very little to the overall accuracy of the Gospel accounts. In this paper, they account for less than 2% of the overall reconstructed text. According to The Jesus Seminar, the most important of the extra-biblical sources are The Gospel of Thomas, Oxyrhynchus 1224, The Egerton Gospel, and a few passages from Eusebius' Ecclesiastical History.

Chapter 2

The Body

Following is a annotated reconstruction of the life and sayings of the Historical Jesus in rough chronological order. It is designed for the purpose of bringing Christians and other interested parties closer to the actual words of the Master. All attempts have been made to strip away accretions of history and theology that were not thought to be part of Jesus' original message. The process for bringing this about is discussed in the previous chapter. In the interest of accuracy, the author has resisted the natural human urge to "fill in the gaps" in places where the evidence was wanting. This results in a narrative that can be rather choppy in parts. However, it seemed wiser to let the reader speculate for him or herself rather than to risk leading them into error with the best of intentions. Above each pericope the reader will find scriptural cross-references for further investigation. Following this chronological narrative is a speculative discussion of the implications of the principal findings of this project.

*"In the beginning was the Word, and the Word was
with God, and the Word was God.
In him was life; and the life was the light of men.
And the light shineth in darkness;
and the darkness comprehended it not.
He came unto his own, and his own received him not.
But as many as received him, to them gave he power to
become the sons of God, even to them that
believe on his name:
Which were born, not of blood, nor of the will of the flesh,
nor of the will of man, but of God.
And the Word was made flesh, and dwelt among us,
and we beheld his glory, the glory as of the only begotten
of the Father, full of grace and truth.[1]*

Introduction[2]

Matthew 2:23; Luke 1:26; 2:4, 34, 46–52; Galatians 2:7–9

This is the true story of Jesus of Nazareth. It is said that Jesus was closer to God than any one who has ever lived. In fact, Jesus himself claimed to be equal with God. This is the story of his life and what he told his friends about God.

In his time, Jesus was known as "Yeshua." Yeshua was a common name in the Middle East and is the same name as "Joshua" in the English tongue. To the ears of the Greek followers of Yeshua, his name sounded like "Jesus," so when they first wrote it down they spelled it J-E-S-U-S. These are the people who wrote our scriptures and were thus the keepers and protectors of our Faith. Jesus frequently referred to himself as the "Son of Man," or "Barnasha" in his native language.

---

1 Probably an early liturgical poem affixed to the Gospel of John. Note the poem does not specifically identify Jesus as "The Word." The "Word" has a long history in the Jewish tradition as the emissary of the wisdom, purpose, and energy of God.

2 The reader will obviously notice the lack of birth narratives. In the oldest accounts, they do not exist, nor are they referred to. The surviving accounts show inconsistencies and are difficult to harmonize. See Appendix 4 for greater detail

Jesus was born into a working class family[3] in northern Israel in 4 B.C., a little over 2000 years ago. He grew up in the town of Nazareth and made his living as a carpenter until his 30th year. Even as a child, he was known for his wisdom, insatiable curiosity, and compassion for others. Jesus had four brothers and at least two sisters. His brother's names were James, Jude, Simon, and Joses. He was closest to his brother James[4] who would eventually be the first person to organize a congregation in the name of his earthly and spiritual brother Jesus. Jesus died by Roman crucifixion in 30 A.D. at the age of 33.

Jesus and John

Mark 1:4–9, 15; Matthew 3:7–11; Luke 3:16

About three years before Jesus started his full-time ministry, his cousin John began preaching in the wilderness near Jerusalem. Jesus would often visit John and talk with him about the meaning of the "Kingdom of God."[5]

John was no ordinary preacher and caused quite a stir with his odd lifestyle and clothing. To show his dedication to God alone, John left behind his life in the city and moved to the country to pray and preach at all times. He even left behind his clothes, and wore only a smock made of camel's hair. John ate whatever he could find, which often included insects and wild honey.

John urged the people to change their ways and to act as people who had had an authentic change-of-heart. Those who were willing to make a permanent change were baptized as a symbol of a new and changed life. John's favorite phrase, which he liked to repeat over-and-over, was "God's Kingdom is Coming! Prepare the way of the Lord!"

---

3 Joseph as Jesus' father only turns up in the conflicting birth accounts of Matthew and Luke which were written more than 50 years after Jesus' death. Paul who was writing only 20 years after the death of Jesus never mentions Joseph. Mary as his mother has only slightly better attestation. There are hints in the Gospels that Jesus was of illegitimate birth and Origen (b. 185 A.D.) relates a legend that Jesus was actually the product of a Roman soldier raping Mary.

4 James is the only apostle referred to as such, specifically, by Paul

5 Many scholars have speculated that Jesus was originally a follower of John. This is not specific in the narrative, but it does seem like a reasonable speculation that fits the available facts.

Some people began to think that John might be someone really special such as an ancient prophet resurrected from the dead, or perhaps an angel. To this, John replied, "Someone more powerful than I will succeed me. This person will be so great and so significant that I wouldn't even feel worthy to tie his shoe. I baptize with water, but he will baptize you with fire!"

Mark 1:10–11; Matthew 3:16; Luke 3:22; John 1:32
One day, Jesus appeared at one of John's baptismal services and requested baptism himself. John at first resisted, but at Jesus' urging, agreed to perform the baptism. For the rest of his life, John remembered this event and the way his heart felt warmed as he came out of the water with Jesus. It was on this day that any of his lingering doubts about his mission disappeared. A few months after this event, the illegitimate "King" of the Hebrews, Herod, had John thrown into prison for remarks he had made about Herod's wife. This would be the beginning of the end of John's short life.

Facing Doubts

Mark 1:12–13; Matthew 4:1–11; Luke 4:1–13
Jesus' official dedication to full-time ministry began with this baptism and his 30th year of life. He left his occupation as a carpenter in Nazareth and would spend the rest of his life serving God and the human race as a traveling teacher, healer, and visionary. But before he could begin, he knew that he had to face his own doubts and temptations. He set off to the barren desert alone for 40 days[6] without food.

Well into his fast, Jesus felt the temptation to use spiritual power to satisfy his physical needs. The devil tormented him with a recurring plea: "Turn these stones to bread. Show your power!" To this Jesus responded, "Human beings are not to live on bread alone, but on every word that comes from the mouth of God." Then an even greater temptation manifested: "Prove you are truly favored by God by jumping off the highest floor of the temple in Jerusalem. All of the people of Jerusalem will see you being saved by the angels of God!" But Jesus calmly replied, "It is not proper to put the Lord to the test." These ex-

---
[6] This is at the outside edge of what is considered survivable. Gandhi came very near death after a 21-day fast.

changes continued for days until Jesus knew the time was right. He exclaimed "Be gone Satan!" and the time for testing was over. His ministry had begun.

First Sermon

Matthew 5:3–6; Luke 6:20–23

Sometime after John's imprisonment, Jesus came to the area of Galilee in Northern Israel proclaiming God's good news. John the Baptist had preached of the coming Kingdom of God, but Jesus declared that it was now here![7] One of his first public sermons was along these lines:

> *Congratulations, you poor!*
> *The Kingdom of God belongs to you.*
> *Congratulations, you who are hungry!*
> *You will have an endless feast.*
> *Congratulations, you who now weep!*
> *You will know endless joy.*

Fishing for People

Mark 1:16–20; 2:14; Matthew 4:18–22; 9:9; Luke 5:27; John 1:35–51

One day, Jesus was walking along the Sea of Galilee and spotted Peter and his brother Andrew casting their fishing nets into the sea. He walked their direction until he was within earshot and then boldly proclaimed, "Become my followers and you will be fishing for people!" Something moved within Peter's heart and he abandoned his work immediately and followed Jesus. Andrew, also moved, followed close behind.

As they walked along together, talking, they caught sight of James (son of Zebedee) and John working on their nets. Right then and there, Jesus called out to them as well. James and John felt compelled to go where Jesus led and so told their father goodbye and followed Jesus.

---

[7] It seems that John the Baptist had an eschatological mission and expected the world to soon end and be followed by, The Kingdom of God. Jesus interpreted this in a spiritual sense: The Kingdom is here now, and God invites you to join.

Mark 1:16–20; 2:14; Matthew 4:18–22; 9:9; Luke 5:27; John 1:35–51

Sometime later, as Jesus was walking along, he came upon a toll booth. Manning the booth was a man named "Levi." Levi was a Jew who made his living collecting tolls for the Romans. Jesus looked him in the eye, smiled, and said, "Levi, come follow me." Levi left his toll booth and his occupation behind and followed Jesus.

Mark 1:29–42; 2:1–12; Luke 4:38–44

Once Jesus was visiting Peter's house when Peter's mother-in-law was sick with a high fever. Jesus touched her hand and the fever disappeared. She then got up and started doing some housework. Jesus' friends were becoming amazed at his wisdom and power.

Luke 17:20–21

Jesus spent a lot of time with his chosen friends doing God's work. At night, Jesus would talk to them about the Kingdom of God. One of his disciples asked, "When will the Kingdom of God arrive? When will it get here?" Jesus replied, "The Kingdom of God does not come by watching for it. You won't say 'Here it is!' or 'There it is over there!' No. The Kingdom of God is spread all over the earth, and yet, people do not see it. Therefore you will not be able to observe the 'coming' of the Kingdom of God. The Kingdom of God is here now, in your presence. It is within and among all of you."

Mark 9:50; Matthew 5:13

"Salt is good and makes food tasty. But what good is it of it becomes bland – if it looses its zing? With what will you make it salty again?"[8]

Spreading the Word

Mark 1:23–39; Luke 4:33–43

One morning, very early, Jesus slipped away from where he was staying with his disciples and walked more than a mile to

---

8 Spong has interpreted this obscure saying to mean something along the following: "You must keep guard of your source of power – always seek the source, the Spirit. There is no real change...no revolution, without it."

find a quiet place to meditate. When his friends woke up, and saw that he was not there, they became worried and began to search for him. After hours of searching they found him and with irritation Peter said, "Everyone has been looking for you!"

Calmly looking up from his prayer, Jesus paused and said, "It is time we moved on and spread our message. We are to go to the neighboring villages as they need our message as badly as this one does." So they went throughout the region of Galilee in Northern Israel, speaking in the churches and driving out demons.

Mark 1:23–39; Luke 4:33–43

At one of the churches they encountered a person with a particularly serious problem. The man had not been able to work in years, and often yelled uncontrollably and shouted obscenities. He was a danger to his family and friends. When the man caught sight of Jesus he screamed, "What are you doing here, Jesus of Nazareth? I know what you are! – A Holy Man of God!"

Jesus, unshaken, firmly responded, "Come out of him – now."

The man convulsed and let out an otherworldly and ear-piercing shriek and then collapsed on the floor. For the first time in years he was free.

Instead of being thankful, some in the audience were afraid of Jesus! "What kind of man is this?," they exclaimed. So, with frequent occurrences such as this, Jesus' fame spread rapidly throughout Galilee and beyond.

Resisting Evil

Mark 1:21–22; Matthew 7:28–29; Luke 4:31–32; John 7:46

Jesus and his followers made their way to Capernaum, a town on the Northern shore of the Sea of Galilee. When Jesus arrived, he went directly to the town synagogue and began to teach. The audience was astonished at his teaching since he taught with authority instead of trying only to make a case for his ideas by quoting scripture.

Matthew 5:39–41; Luke 6:29–30

At one of his lectures, he addressed the audience as follows: "In your dealings with the world be as sly as snakes but as innocent as doves." "But, Teacher," a disciple replied, "how can we show love to those who are trying to hurt or kill us?" Jesus replied, "The best way to deal with violence is to not react violently to an evil person. In fact, if someone should slap you on the right cheek, give them your left as well. When you react to violence you get drawn into the violence and risk doing evil as well. If someone threatens to sue you for your coat, give them your coat and your shirt as well. And, even if the Roman officers force you to carry their goods an entire mile, then walk a second mile as well – all without anger. Do not feed the energy of a violent and evil person." "These sayings are hard to understand, and even harder to do," claimed another of Jesus' disciples, to which Jesus replied, "You must struggle to get in through the narrow door. Many will try to get in, but few will persevere. And I will tell you an even more difficult saying along these lines. Unless a person completely dedicates himself to the quest for God, that is, puts God ahead of all other relationships; mother, brother, sisters, he cannot be my true disciple."

Mark 1:29–42; 2:1–12; Luke 4:38–44

Once, Jesus was touring the countryside when a person with leprosy came up to him. The man fell to his knees pleading and begged Jesus, "Please make me well." Jesus seemed irritated,[9] but stretched out his arm and touched him saying, "You are clean!" Immediately the leprosy disappeared and the man was completely well.

Mark 1:29–42; 2:1–12; Luke 4:38–44

Back in Capernaum, the word got around that Jesus was home. Many people crowded around so that there was no longer any room – even outside the door. Nevertheless, Jesus began to speak to them all. There were some people who showed up carrying their paralytic friend on a stretcher. Since they couldn't get in the door, they climbed up on the roof, removed some of the ceiling panels and began to lower their paralytic friend down to Jesus to be healed. When Jesus saw their simple faith and trust, he said (looking at the paralyzed man), "My child, your sins are

---

9 Some of the oldest and most reliable Greek texts have "irritated" instead of the more familiar "moved with compassion." Since it is harder to imagine that a scribe would change "compassion" to "irritation" than the other way around, the author has assumed "irritated" to be the original meaning.

forgiven." Some in the audience wondered to themselves, "Why does he say such things? Doesn't he know that only God can forgive sins?" Jesus sensed their doubts and addressed them: "Why are you entertaining such questions? Is it easier to say 'your sins are forgiven,' or 'pick up your mat and walk'?"

Then, the man got up, picked up his mat, and walked out as everyone looked on. Most of the crowd became ecstatic and spontaneously erupted in praise to God. One proclaimed, "We have never seen anything like this before!"

Eating with Sinners

Mark 2:15–17; Matthew 9:10–13; Luke 5:29–32

One time, Jesus was attending a large banquet. When he got his plate and sat down, he chose to sit in the section with the tax collectors and other people of bad reputation. When he got up again, a group of Pharisees pulled him aside and asked him to defend his odd behavior. "Why are you eating with those sinners?" they asked.

Jesus smiled and responded, "The able-bodied don't need a doctor, do they? It's the sick that do. I did not come to help the religious folk, but only the 'sinners.'" Despite his kind and well thought out answer, these Pharisees were still visibly perturbed and went on their way, scowling.

Mark 2:18–22; Matthew 9:14–15; Luke 5:33–34

On another occasion, a would-be disciple told Jesus that he was uncomfortable with the fact that Jesus didn't fast regularly as John the Baptist and the Pharisees did. Jesus answered, "The groom's friends do not fast while the groom is still around. You cannot expect them to fast when the celebration is still going on and they are all together enjoying one another's company. However the real issue is that people don't like to change their old customs and habits. Nobody wants to switch from their favorite food or drink that they have eaten all their life and try something new on a mere whim. People feel the same way about new ideas as they do new foods. They don't like change — sometimes to their great detriment.

Lord of the Sabbath

Mark 2:23-28; Matthew 12:1-8; Luke 6:1-5

One day, on their way back from the Synagogue on Saturday, Jesus and his disciples took a short-cut home through a field of grain. As they were hungry, they picked some of the heads of the grain and popped them in their mouths as a snack. Coming up behind them were some Pharisees who were annoyed at the disciples and Jesus. According to the Pharisees' interpretation of the Old Testament, work was not allowed on the Sabbath and to them, picking a head of grain was "work." So they yelled ahead at Jesus, "Why do you allow your followers to break the laws of the Sabbath day?!"

> *Jesus said to them:*
> *The Sabbath day was created for Humans;*
> *Not humans for the Sabbath day.*
> *The Sabbath day of worship was ordained to enlighten*
> *Mankind,*
> *Not to be a senseless burden.*
> *However, the Son of Man is Lord even over the Sabbath.*

Mark 3:1-5; Matthew 12:9-13; Luke 6:6-10

That evening Jesus returned to the Synagogue and there met a man with a crippled hand. The Pharisees were still irritated about the incident earlier in the day, so they watched Jesus carefully to see if he would try and heal the man. They were hoping to get him on more "violations" of the Sabbath day-of-rest. To their surprise, Jesus announced loudly to the crippled man, "Come up here to the podium with me." Then he asked the audience, "Is it permissible to do good or evil on the Sabbath day? Is it better on the Sabbath day to save life or to destroy it?"

But the Pharisees stood their ground and did not reply. Jesus looked right at the Pharisees and said to the crippled man, "Hold out your hand!"

The man did as Jesus said and his hand become normal.

Good Things

Matthew 5:44–47; Luke 6:27–33

Jesus set up camp near the shoreline, and with a huge crowd gathering about him he began to teach. "Love your enemies. If you only love those who love you back, what does that prove? Even the worst of sinners love those who love them. And if you only do good things for people who do good things to you, what does that prove? Even the worst of sinners meet this minimum requirement."

And then he added, "God causes the sun to rise on both the bad and the good. Likewise he sends the rain to both the just and the unjust. Just look around you! God is generous to both the ungrateful and the wicked."

Matthew 7:9–11; Luke 11:11–13

He continued, "Would anyone among you hand your child a stone when he asked for bread? Would you hand him a snake if he was asking for a fish? Of course you wouldn't! If mere mortals, as unscrupulous as they are, still know how to give appropriate gifts to their children, isn't it even more likely that the Father in Heaven will give good things to those who ask of him?"

Mark 3:22–26; Matthew 12:24–36; Luke 11:15–23

Once, during one of his talks, a skeptic yelled, "He can drive out demons because he is league with Beelzebul, the prince of all demons!" Others would test him by demanding a sign from heaven. However, Jesus always knew what they were thinking, and he knew the heart of man. He responded to the neigh-sayers: "Any government that is divided within is soon devastated. A house divided soon falls. If Satan is divided, by attacking himself (supposedly through me), then how can his kingdom endure? Why would he do something not in his best interest? By the way, if I drive out demons in Beelzebul's name, in whose name do your people drive them out? Therefore, the character of those men will say a lot about your own motives. But what if I am really using the legitimate power of God? Wouldn't that be a clear signal that the Kingdom of God had arrived? I tell you this – I have started a wildfire on this earth; and I will guard it until it blazes."

Matthew 12:43-45; Luke 21:1-4

"When an unclean spirit leaves a person, it wanders through deserts looking for a place to rest. When it doesn't find one, it says to itself, 'I'll return to the place I left.' So it returns and finds the place swept and clean. Then it goes and finds its friends, who are even more evil, and they all settle into the comfortable arrangement. So you see, this person is even worse off then when he started."

Mark 3:27; Matthew 12:29; Luke 11:21-22

"No one can enter the house of a strong man and steal his things unless he first ties him up. Only then does the looting begin."

Growth

Mark 3:20-21;31-35; Matthew 12:46-50; Luke 8:19-21; John 10:20

Jesus and his disciples traveled back to his hometown to get some rest and prepare for the next phase of his mission. They were staying in a house that belonged to one of Jesus' relatives. However, somehow word got out that Jesus was staying in town and desperate people began to crowd outside the house. Some folks were there to be healed. Some just wanted to see what this famous man, "Jesus," looked like. Others didn't like Jesus. They thought he was crazy and wanted him gone! So, the crowd was very rowdy. By the time Jesus' mother Mary arrived with his brothers James, Jude, Simon, and Joses, they could barely get to the front door. One of the disciples heard Mary's voice outside and told Jesus, "Sir. Your mother and brothers are here!"

In response, Jesus said, "Who are my mother and brothers?" And looking around the crowd of disciples in the house, making eye contact with each of them, he added, "Right here are my mother and brothers. Whoever thirsts for the Will of God – he or she is my brother, sister, or mother!"

Mark 4:1-8; Matthew 13:1-8; Luke 8:5-8

Returning to his encampment by the sea, he prepared to preach to the crowds. He got into a boat and sailed away from the shore, facing the growing throng. This day he would share with them several parables.

26 *Jesus Alone*

"A farmer went out to plant his seed. While he was sowing, some seed fell to the wayside and was eaten up by birds. Other seed fell upon the rocky soil and plants sprang right up. However, because the soil had no depth, and the roots were short, the plants were soon scorched to death by the sun. Some of the farmer's seed fell among the thorns. When the plants came up they were choked and produced no fruit. Finally, some of the seed fell on rich healthy soil and produced fruit. This seed sprouted and grew with a significant yield."

"Even when growing, growth is gradual. First someone plants a seed. Then the person checks its progress every day. The seed sprouts and then matures, although the farmer still cannot see it. Finally a tiny shoot is visible above the ground, then a head, then a fully mature plant. And when the grain is fully ripe the farmer gets his sickle because it is harvest time."[10]

Kingdom of God

Matthew 22:2–13; Luke 14:15–24

Jesus liked to tell stories to illustrate spiritual truths. At one setting he shared the following parable: "A man was planning a big party and invited many guests. At 4:30pm, he sent his butler to tell the guests that the feast was ready. But one by one they made lame excuses why they couldn't come. Angered by the lack of appreciation, the man told his butler to go out in the streets and invite everyone. But even then, there were still seats available at the table. Then the man said: 'Invite everyone in the world; anyone who can walk or drag themselves to the party. I insist that my house be filled!'"

Mark 4:30–32; Matthew 13:31–32; Luke 13:18–19

"Let me tell you what the Kingdom of God is. It is like a small seed. Even though it is tiny, it becomes something great when it falls upon prepared soil. It grows into a large tree that becomes a shelter for the birds of the sky. Or one could say the Kingdom is like a small amount of yeast mixed into many pounds of dough. You cannot see its effects until the bread begins to rise."

---
10 A clearly "Karmic" parable.

"Or, the Kingdom of God is like a person who fantasized about winning a great race. Day after day the man would go running in the field; simulating the race to come, to see if he would have the strength to endure when the time came."[11]

Matthew 13:44

Later that day, Jesus said, "The Kingdom of God is like a valuable treasure hidden in a field. When someone finds it, they cover it back up and spend every cent they have to buy the field." And after a pause, he began again, "The Kingdom of Heaven is like a merchant who had a very large inventory and then came across a beautiful rare pearl. That merchant was wise; he sold everything he had…his entire inventory…to buy that single pearl."

Mark 6:10; Luke 10:5-8

Jesus gave the following advice to his apostles who were traveling to spread the Good News of the Kingdom of God: "When you enter a house, say, 'Peace to this house.' Stay at the one house and eat whatever food they are kind enough to provide. Don't complain and don't keep moving from house to house."

Mark 6:1-6; Matthew 13:54-58

Jesus left that place and traveled back to his hometown along with many of his disciples. On the Sabbath day, he went to the synagogue, as was his custom, and began to lecture. Many who heard were amazed at his insight and wisdom. "Where is he getting all this?" they would ask themselves. "I thought he was the son of a carpenter, a working class laborer?" And because of their prejudices and presuppositions, they had a hard time listening to him. Some in the crowd even acted resentful or jealous. Jesus stopped and addressed their doubt: "No prophet goes without respect except in his home country and among his relatives!" Because of the negative feelings he could not perform a single miracle there, except the curing of a few minor illnesses. He did travel all around the area though, and taught whomever would listen about the Kingdom of God.

---

[11] A paraphrase from a quip in the Gospel of Thomas not found in the canonical Gospels. Curiously, Paul also uses similar metaphors (*e.g.* I Corinthians 9:24) that may go back to his knowledge of Jesus' most ancient sayings, now lost.

Mark 5:24-34; Matthew 9:20-22; Luke 8:43-48

In one place where Jesus was staying, a large crowd gathered. So many wanted to be near him that it was difficult for him to walk. In the crowd was a desperate woman who had internal bleeding. The woman slowly worked her way through the throng and touched Jesus on the back, hoping for a miracle cure. When she touched him, she suddenly felt different inside. The bleeding had stopped the instant she touched Jesus and she was completely healed. Jesus stopped what he was doing, turned and looked at her and said, "Daughter, your faith has made you whole."[12]

Wisdom's Children

Matthew 11:16-19; Luke 7:31-35

At one particular gathering, Jesus responded to some hecklers with the following lesson: "What is this world like? What is it really like? The people of this world are like little children at the park playing together and singing a song:

> *We played the flute for you,*
> *but you wouldn't dance;*
> *then we sang a sad song,*
> *but you wouldn't cry.*

My cousin John appeared in this world refusing fine foods and wine and you said he was 'too extreme.' But the Son of Man has not observed any particular dietary regimen and eats the same foods as his disciples and you say that he is a 'loose-liver' and a friend to scumbags and criminals. But I tell you, Wisdom is justified by her children."

Elijah Reborn

Mark 6:14-29; Matthew 14:1-12

News of Jesus' wisdom and teaching reached the ears of Herod the King. Many were saying that Jesus was the great Old

---

[12] One of many examples of Jesus attributing healing power to the one that is healed, rather than to himself.

Testament prophet Elijah reborn. Others thought he was the one to re-initiate the age of prophets that had ended with the great prophets years before.[13]

Earlier, King Herod had had John arrested and thrown into the dungeon. Herod's wife, Herodias, wanted John dead because he had preached publicly about the immorality of her divorce from her previous husband as well as Herod's mistreatment of his previous wife. However, deep down inside, Herod was afraid to kill John. Part of him wondered if John might actually be speaking for God, and if he were, if killing him might not bring God's curse.

On national holidays, Herod often threw elaborate parties for his wealthy friends and other high ranking officials. At one of these parties, his wife Herodias asked her daughter Salome to dance for the people there. Herod was so impressed with her show that he promised her up to half of his kingdom as a reward. He said this out loud in front of all his friends and supporters.

After consulting with her mother, Salome announced to the crowd, "I want John the Baptist's head delivered on a platter immediately!" Herod's jaw dropped in shock, but he realized that as King he could not back down after making such a bold promise in public. Herod glanced sadly to his left at his personal bodyguards and said, "Let it be done." Therefore, the guards notified the executioner and this evil deed was added to the other many evil deeds Herod had done.

Later, the news of John's death was brought to Jesus as he was preaching to a crowd. He shared the news of John's death and the mood became very sad. Then, after a long pause, Jesus announced, "When you went out to the wilderness to see John preach, what did you go to see? Grass blowing in the wind? What did you really go out to see? A man dressed in an expensive suit? But wait! Those who wear fine clothes are found in fancy buildings with a corner office."

---

13 Even in Jesus' time this would have been considered "Ancient" history. Many believed that the Age of Prophets ended more than 500 years before Jesus' birth.

Fruit

Mark 7:1–16; Matthew 15:10–11

Jesus was eating a large public meal with his disciples and friends. A group of Pharisees, who had heard rumors about Jesus, came to the meal in hopes of seeing what Jesus was like. Some of them wanted to see if they could catch him using a scriptural inaccuracy. Others among them were just curious. As they were mulling around, they noticed that some of the Jesus' disciples were eating without washing their hands. One of the Pharisees approached Jesus and questioned him directly, "Why aren't your disciples living up to the traditions of the elders? Why do you let them eat bread with defiled hands?" Now the Pharisaical tradition of hand washing had nothing to do with cleanliness. It was a ceremonial washing that they believed had been handed down by authoritative church leaders.

Jesus clapped him hands to get the attention of the crowd and addressed everyone on this matter: "Everyone listen, and please try hard to understand. It is not what goes into your body that defiles you. It is what comes out of your heart. Rituals can be useful, but they do not prove that a person's heart is pure. And the lack of them certainly does not prove that someone is unfit to worship God. There are those who ceremonially wash the outside of all of their cups. Why do they not also wash the inside? Wash the inside first. Then the outside will be clean as well."

"If you want to know what the heart of a person is really like, look at the fruit they produce. Good trees produce good fruit and bad trees produce bad fruit. People do not pick grapes from thorn trees or figs from thistles."[14]

Do Unto Others

Mark 8:11–13; Matthew 12:38–40; 16:1–9; Luke 11:29–30

One time when Jesus was speaking to a crowd some members of the Pharisees were present. To test his authority one of them asked Jesus to cause a miraculous sign in the sky. With a frustrated look, Jesus replied, "Why does this generation insist on a sign? I solemnly promise, this generation won't get a sign!"

---
[14] Another clearly "Karmic" parable.

Then Jesus simply turned around, walked back to his boat and crossed to the other side.

Mark 7:24–30; Matthew 15:21–28

Jesus then made his way to the seaside town of Tyre, which is just across the Northwestern-most border of Israel. Jesus attempted to travel quietly so as to not be mobbed by the crowds. Nevertheless, a woman whose daughter had an unclean spirit managed, after great effort, to track him down. When she finally saw Jesus in person, she fell at his feet. This particular woman spoke Greek and not the native Aramaic tongue of Jesus. She was also a Phoenician by ethnicity who resided in Syria. The woman begged Jesus incessantly to heal her troubled daughter. Jesus said "Shouldn't the children be fed first? Is it fitting to take the bread from the children's mouths and throw it to the dogs?"

The woman replied, without missing a beat, "Even the dogs get to eat the scraps dropped by the children!"

Jesus then replied, "Because of your persistence and faith your daughter is healed. When you get home you will find her well."

When the woman got home she found her daughter fully recovered and sitting comfortably on the couch.

Mark 10:13–15; Matthew 18:3, 19:13–15; Luke 18:15–17

Frequently, parents would bring children to Jesus to receive a blessing. Jesus was fond of children and didn't seem to mind stopping what he was doing to spend time with them. Sometimes Jesus' adult friends would shoo the kids away, but Jesus corrected them: "Let the children come to me. Do not get in their way. You must realize that the Kingdom of God belongs to people just like that. In fact, if a person cannot accept God like a child does, they cannot really accept God at all."

Matthew 18:23–34

"The Kingdom of God can be compared to a high-ranking ruler who decided to settle accounts with his underlings. A debtor was brought to him who owed ten million dollars. Since he couldn't pay it back, the ruler ordered him to be sold into slavery along with his wife and children. In absolute desperation, the employee fell down on his knees before the ruler and begged, weeping, 'Be patient with me. I promise you, I will repay every cent.' Moved with compassion the ruler let the man go and completely cancelled his great debt. But, as soon as he was free, this same fellow who had received so much grace, saw one of his servants who owed him only 100 dollars, and grabbed him by the neck! He demanded, 'Pay me what you owe me if you value your life!' The servant begged for patience. But the employee who had received so much consideration by the ruler didn't even listen to the poor servant – in fact, he used his connections to have him thrown into debtor's prison. The other servants couldn't believe what they saw and word soon got back to the ruler. The employee who had owed the ten million dollars was summoned by the ruler once again. The ruler said, 'You wicked, wicked man! I showed you great compassion in forgiving your debt and yet you were harsh with this poor servant of yours. Shouldn't you have at least shown the same compassion to this man that you had received?' The ruler was so angry that he revoked the man's pardon and threw him in prison until his family could repay every last penny."

John 8:3–11

Jesus' lecture was interrupted by a gang of religious zealots. They approached Jesus, screaming and yelling that they had caught a woman in the act of adultery. The crowd cleared a path for them and they threw the woman at Jesus' feet. The man who brought her said, "Teacher, this woman was caught in the act of adultery. The Bible commands that such a woman should be pelted with stones until dead. What would you have us do?" Jesus' enemies said this in an attempt to trap him into breaking one of the technicalities in the religious law, but Jesus saw right through it.

Jesus stooped down and began drawing in sand with his finger. Everyone in the crowd anxiously awaited his words. After several minutes, Jesus stood up and proclaimed, "Whoever in this crowd has never committed a sin may throw the first stone." Again, he squatted on the ground and seemed to write with his finger.

The crowd began to slowly disperse. The oldest men in the crowd left first, but eventually everyone had gone leaving Jesus alone with the accused woman.

Jesus looked at her kindly and asked, "Where has everyone gone? Is there no one left to condemn you?"

She replied, "No one, sir."

"Then I do not do not condemn you either," Jesus said. "You are free to go, but, sin no more."

Riches

Luke 12:16-20; 18:24-25

It was widely believed during the time of Jesus that riches were a sign of God's favor. Jesus addressed this in one of his lectures. He began, "The rich are not any closer to God than anyone else. In fact, they have a very difficult time entering the Kingdom of God! I tell you the truth — It is easier to squeeze a large rope through the eye of a needle than it is for a rich person to enter God's domain.[15] This is because no servant can be a slave to two masters. Without a doubt, the slave will hate one and love the other, or be devoted to one and disdain the other. You cannot serve both God and money."

Luke 12:16-20; 18:24-25

"Consider the following: There was a rich man who had a great deal of money. He said to himself, 'I shall invest my money so that I can fill my mansion and storehouse with stuff for me. Then I will use any extra to pad and protect my lifestyle. Nothing will hurt me!' But that very night he had a heart attack and died. None of the stuff he worked for went with him. He who has ears to hear should listen!"

Matthew 5:42; Luke 6:34

"If you have money to give, don't lend it at interest. Give it to someone from whom you will not get it back. If you only give money out of hope of gaining more, what merit it there in that? Even outlaws and sinners lend to their own if they can make a buck out of it."

Mark 8:35; Luke 17:33

"If you try to hang on to material life too tightly you will forfeit it, but, if you forfeit the transient material world you will live! Do not attach yourself to things which do not last."[16]

---

15 The words for "rope" and "camel" are very similar to each other in the original languages. It seems reasonable to assume the words were switched or confused early on in the history of the text. Thus the current author has substituted the word that seems more likely in the context.

16 A wonderful pericope of the Eastern concept of "Non-Attachment."

Matthew 8:19–22; Luke 9:57–58

One day as Jesus and his followers were traveling down the road they came upon a group of men. One of the men listened carefully to Jesus and showed great interest in his cause. He said to Jesus, "I'll follow wherever you go!" Jesus replied to him, "Foxes have dens, and birds have nests; but the Son of Man has nowhere to rest his head." Then, to the group of men, Jesus simply said, "Follow me." But one of the men said, "I want to become your disciple, but I must wait until my Father dies; I have a responsibility to him as well." But Jesus said to him, "Let the dead bury their own dead; but you come and join me in announcing the Kingdom of God."

Your Neighbor

Mark 12:28–37; Matthew 22:34–40; Luke 10:25–28

On another occasion, a learned theologian of the Pharisee party sought out Jesus in sincerity and asked him the following heart-felt question: "Sir, I see you are a wise teacher, admired by the people. Of all the many commandments in the Old Testament, which one would you say was the most important of all?" Without missing a beat, Jesus replied by paraphrasing the Jewish "Shema" from the book of Deuteronomy: "'Hear O Israel, the LORD our God is one LORD. And you shall love the LORD your God with all of your heart, and with all of your soul, with all of your mind, and all of your strength.' And the second greatest commandment is this, 'You shall love your neighbor as yourself.' There are no commandments in the entire Old Testament more important than these two. If you keep these, you will keep all of the others automatically. These commandments lead to eternal salvation." But the man did not give up so easily. He replied, "But sir, what do you mean by 'neighbor?'"

Jesus replied, "Consider this: A certain man was traveling from Jerusalem to Jericho. Unfortunately for him, robbers were hiding in the hills and they attacked him, took his belongings, and beat him nearly to death. They left his bruised and bloody body by the roadside. About 30 minutes after the robbery, a Priest came down the road. When he saw the man, he went way around him so that the man would not make him ritually 'unclean.' A little while later a temple assistant was coming down the road. He too saw the man, but didn't want to get involved. Finally a man from Samaria, a despised 'half-breed' Jew, was coming down the road. When he saw the poor beaten man he was moved with compassion. He ran to him and bandaged his wounds and treated them with medicine. Then he put the man on his own donkey and walked beside him all the way into town. He took him to a motel and paid the man's bill. He left some extra money at the front office, just in case the man needed it to get back on his feet. Now I ask you: Which of these three men in the story was a 'neighbor' to the injured man?" The learned Pharisee replied, "The one who showed him compassion." Jesus replied, "Go and do likewise."

Seeking
Mark 11:25-26; Matthew 6:7-15; 7:12; Luke 6:31; 11:1-4

Jesus prayed frequently and often sought out solitary places to pray. One time, one of his disciples asked him about the "secret" of prayer. Jesus responded: "When you pray, keep it simple. It isn't necessary to make a show or repeat long sentences." However, Jesus' followers insisted that he teach them a specific prayer to recite. "Alright – pray along these lines:

> *Great and Holy Father,*
> *May you always be on our minds.*
> *Give us our bread for today.*
> *Bring about your Kingdom on Earth,*
> *As it already is in Heaven.*
> *Give us strength to forgive other people,*
> *So that we may be at peace ourselves.*
> *Amen.*[17]

If you sincerely want to be forgiven by God, then become a person of forgiveness. Practice forgiving others and you will thus find forgiveness yourself. And, when you pray, go into a room alone and shut the door behind you."

---
17 Jesus seems reticent to recommend a static prayer. When he does it is almost entirely praise and basic needs. It ends with a very Karmic admonition to forgive others as a pre-condition to finding forgiveness for oneself.

Luke 10:30–35

Jesus had been staying in the town of Jericho Ariha, which is East of Jerusalem near the Jordan river. As he was heading out of town, he noticed a blind beggar named Bartimaeus, sitting by the side of the road. As Jesus approached, Bartimaeus shouted with all his might, "Jesus, Son of David, have mercy on me!" Those around him told him to keep quiet, but he only shouted all the louder, "Son of David! Have mercy on me!" Jesus walked quickly to where the man was. When Jesus arrived, the man threw off his cloak and jumped to his feet. Jesus said, "What is it you want me to do for you?" The man answered, "Rabbi, I want to see again!" Jesus said to him, "You can now be on your way. Your faith has made you whole." And immediately he regained his sight and began to follow Jesus down the road.

Turning to the crowd, Jesus said, "People don't light a lamp and then put it under a basket. But rather, they put it upon a lamp stand where it can provide light for everyone around. And a giant city on the top of a mountain cannot be concealed."

Matthew 7:7–8; Luke 11:9–13

"Ask and it will be given you; seek, and you will find; knock on the door, and it will be opened for you. You can be sure that everyone who asks receives; everyone who seeks finds; and when a person knocks, the door is opened."

Matthew 7:1–5; Luke 6:37–42

After a pause he concluded, "There are those who see the speck of wood-dust in their friend's eye, but cannot see the log in their own eye! Take the log out of your eye and then you will see well enough to help your friend. Don't waste your energy judging other people. Work on the condition of your own heart. Remember – the standard you use to judge others will be the standard by which you yourself are judged."

Matthew 6:25–30; Luke 12:22–31

"Don't spend your energy worrying about life – what you are going to eat, or about clothing for your body. There is so much more to living than food and clothing. Think about the birds. They don't plant or harvest, nor do they have storehouses or barns. Yet God feeds them. Don't you realize that you are worth so much more than birds? God even knows the number of the hairs upon your head.

Can you add even one hour to your life by fretting about it? So if you can't even do that, why worry about anything? Think of the wildflowers. They neither worry nor sweat. Yet, even Solomon was never dressed as fine as them. If God so takes care of the plants in the field which are here today and gone tomorrow, is it not surely more likely that he has your best welfare in mind? Gratitude should replace worry in the mind of one truly seeking God."

Luke 13:6–9

Jesus then told the following parable: "A man had an apple tree planted in his backyard. He came out looking for fruit one day but couldn't find any apples on his tree. So he said to his gardener, 'I have been waiting three years for apples to grow on this tree. Cut it down! It is only wasting space in my backyard.' But the gardener replied, 'Sir. Please give it just one more year. I will work overtime on it with fertilizer, extra water, and care. I'll bet you anything it will produce some apples next year. But if not, I will cut it down then.'"

Matthew 18:12–13; Luke 15:4–9

Jesus posited the following question to a crowd: "If a woman has ten silver coins and misplaces only one of them, won't she keep searching until she finds it? In fact, she will frantically look in every corner of the house with her flashlight until the coin is found. Then the woman will call her friends to let them know the good news! "Celebrate with me," she will say, "the coin I lost has been found!"

If a shepherd owns a hundred sheep and only one of them wonders off, what will he do? He will leave the ninety-nine at home and go looking for the little lost sheep. When he finds it, he will lift it up on him shoulders and smile. And, like the woman with the lost coin, he will call his friends to help him celebrate his discovery!"

Mark 10:31; Matthew 20:1–15

On one occasion, he opened his sermon with the words, "The last will be first and the first shall be last." He then went on to share this parable, "The Kingdom of Heaven is like a boss who went out at 7:00 A.M. to hire laborers for his farm. He agreed to pay them $50 for the day's work, and sent them into the fields. At about 9:00 A.M. he went into town to visit the store and saw some young men bumming around outside. He told them that he had work for them and that he would pay them a fair wage to work his fields. They agreed and went back to the farm with him. He continued this process of going into town looking for laborers all day. Many men were hired. The last group joined the crew after 5:00 P.M. At 6:00 P.M., the whistle blew, and the men lined up to be paid. Everyone who worked that day received $50, one at a time. The men who worked all day were astonished! 'Why did you pay those guys who worked only an hour the same amount that you paid us?' The boss replied, 'I agreed to pay you $50, did I not? Did I wrong you? Isn't it my prerogative to pay my workers any wage I want? Your problem is that you are envious and jealous, when I am only trying to show generosity!"

Luke 15:11–32

On a different occasion, he shared this parable:

Once there was a man with two teenage sons. The younger of the two came to his father and said, "Father. I am nearly an adult and ready to leave home and start my own life. Please give me my inheritance in advance." The father agreed and went ahead and divided a large amount of money between the two boys.

Not long after that, the younger son packed his things and left for the big city to find himself. But when he arrived he soon got in with the wrong crowd and behaved recklessly. Within six months he had spent his entire inheritance and had nothing to show for it. Unfortunately for him, just when he was approaching "rock bottom," the economy hit a terrible slump and there were no jobs available. In some places people couldn't even get enough to eat. He began to actually fear for his life and was overwhelmed with guilt. He finally managed to get a menial job as a pig-herder on the outskirts of the city. He became so hungry that he would sometimes steal some of the slop from the pigs and eat it himself.

Then one day, he came to his senses. He realized that even the servants that worked at his father's mansion had it better than he did! So he formulated a plan: "I will go to my father on my knees, and beg for his forgiveness. I will then pledge myself to him for life, as one of his servants." So the man stopped what he was doing and began the long journey back to his father's house.

While he was still far off in the distance, his father saw him coming. His heart melted at the sight of his lost son and he ran out to meet him. He threw his arms around his son and kissed him with joy. And with that, the prodigal son said, "Father, I have sinned against God and against you. I no longer deserve to be called your son. Please consider me as one of your servants."

However, the Father commanded his slaves, "Quickly! Get my finest coat and put it around his shoulders! Bring him my favorite gold ring from the top of my dresser! Tell the cooks to prepare our yearly feast early — today! We have something much more important to celebrate than the harvest! This son of mine was dead; but has come back to life. He was lost, but now he is found!" And everyone began to celebrate.

Now the older son, the one who had stayed and had been working daily for the Father, was out in the field working while all of this was going on. As he dragged his tired body home he heard music and dancing at the main house. He asked a servant boy what was going on.

The boy told him, "Your long lost brother is back! He has changed his ways and his heart! And, your father has thrown a great party to celebrate his return."

The older son grew angry and refused to go to the party. His father saw him outside pouting and went out to talk with him. He said to his father, "All these years I have slaved for you. I have been a good son. I have not wasted your money or disobeyed your orders. However, you have never once thrown a party for me. But when my deadbeat brother shows up you throw this feast!?"

To this the father replied, "My son; you have always been at my side. Everything that I have has been yours. But we had to celebrate! Your brother was dead, but he has come back to life. He was lost, but is now found."

Luke 16:1-8

Shortly after announcing that he would soon be traveling to Jerusalem, Jesus shared the following parable with his disciples: "There once was a business owner whose Chief Executive Officer had been accused of squandering the owner's capital. The business' owner called him into his office and said, 'What is this I have heard about your behavior? I am ordering an audit of your files effective immediately. If things aren't on the up-and-up, you will be most certainly terminated!'

The C.E.O. was terrified. He thought to himself, 'What am I going to do? I have invested my life into this career. I am too proud to go on welfare.' So he began to formulate a plan. The C.E.O. called in each of the business owner's debtors. He said to the first, 'How much do you owe the company?' The man replied, 'Five thousand dollars.' The C.E.O. said to him, 'Here is your invoice – let's just make it $2,500 and call it even.' Then the C.E.O. called in another debtor who owed ten thousand dollars to the company. 'If you give me $8,000 today, I'll tear up your invoice.'" When word got back to the owner, he actually praised the dishonest C.E.O. for his shrewdness; for the children of this world in their time and place are wiser than the children of light.

Approaching Jerusalem

Matthew 6:6; Luke 18:9-14

Jesus began, "When you give to charity, don't let your left hand know what your right hand is doing. Give out of the overflow of your heart." However, his disciples prompted him for further explanation. He continued, "Consider the following: Two men went to church to pray. One was a high-ranking teacher of Moses' law; a Pharisee. The other was a despised tax collector – a traitor to his own people. The Pharisee prayed to God thus: 'I thank you God that I am not a sinner like everyone else. I thank you that I am not like that tax collector sitting there on the back pew. After all, I fast twice per week and always give a portion of my income to the church.'

But the tax collector sat all by himself and didn't even dare to look up at the altar. He beat his chest in despair and said 'Oh God, have mercy upon me – sinner that I am.'

I tell you the truth! The second man went home acquitted but the first did not! For those who promote themselves will be brought down, but those who demote themselves will be raised up. Consider this – in reality there is nothing now veiled that will not be eventually unveiled. There is nothing hidden that will not come to light. God sees the heart of man."

Mark 10:35–45; Luke 22:24–27; John 10:34; Psalm 82

As Jesus and his followers approached Jerusalem, James and John were discussing Jesus' coming kingdom among themselves. Finally, John worked up the courage to address Jesus directly. "When you come into your kingdom, can I sit at your right hand and James at your left? Can we be co-rulers with you in the coming kingdom?" Jesus replied, "You don't even know what you are asking! Do you really think you can walk with me all the way to the end? Do you really believe that you can also drink from this cup that I will have to drink from?" And with a loving pause and a shake of the head he continued, "Such things are not mine to give but belong to the Father alone." The others in the group overheard John's question and became very angry at his arrogance and secrecy. Jesus then addressed the entire group: "As you well know, those who rule this world do it with an iron hand. They believe that giving orders and having lots of followers are the measure of leadership. But they are wrong. If you want to be truly great then focus on serving others, not on giving orders. The greatest of all will be the one who is the servant of all. Let me be clear. I was not born so that I could be waited on hand-and-foot. Nor have I aspired to lead by force. In fact, before long, I will give my very life as a martyr: An example for many to follow.[18] The spark of the divine rests in us all.[19] Remember the psalm Asaph sang for the Lord (Psalm 82):

> *They know not, neither will they understand.*
> *They walk on in darkness:*
> *As the foundation of the Earth is out of course.*
> *I have said, "You all are gods,*

---

[18] I am following the suggested interpretation of the Greek outlined in the previous chapters.

[19] "Ye are all gods"

and children of the Sovereign Lord."
But you all will die as mere men,
The workers as well as the princes.
Arise, O God. Judge this earth!
Thy Kingdom Come!

Mark 8:22-24

Jesus and his followers arrived in Bethsaida and Jesus began to teach. A blind man was brought to Jesus with the help of his friends. The blind man pleaded with Jesus to touch him and make him well. Jesus stopped what he was doing and took the blind man by the hand and led him out of the village. Jesus spat into the blind man's eyes, placed his hands on him and asked, "Do you see anything?" The man blinked and then squinted answering, "I see people walking around, I think. They look like trees." Jesus put his hand on the man's eyes again. The man strained to focus and then his expression changed. "Even the distant things are now clear," the man said.

John 5:2-9

In Jerusalem, by the Sheep Gate, there is a pool known as "Bethzatha" in the Hebrew language. It has five colonnades among which numerous handicapped people would gather. There was one man there who had been crippled for 38 years. Jesus saw him and realized that he had been there a long time. Jesus approached him and asked, "Do you want to get well?" The man replied, "Sir, I don't have anyone to put me in the pool when the water is agitated. Every time I try to make my way someone beats me to it." Moved with compassion Jesus responded, "Get up, pick up your mat and walk." The man recovered at once and picked up his mat as Jesus said.

Mark 11:15-17; Matthew 19:45-46; 21:12-13

Jesus and his followers arrived in Jerusalem for the last time. As planned, he showed up at the temple and made a bold statement by driving out the money changers and sellers in the temple. He addressed them directly in front of the crowds, "The scriptures say, 'Mine house shall be called a house of prayer for all people,' but you have turned it into a den of thieves!"

Mark 12:13–17

Jesus' actions in Jerusalem led to many public disputes with community leaders. Once, they showed Jesus a gold coin and said to him, "The Roman government demands taxes from us." Jesus replied, "Give to the emperor what belongs to the emperor, and give to God what belongs to God."

Mark 4:25; Matthew 25:14–28; Luke 19:13–27

On another occasion he began his sermon with these words: "Those who have will be given more; those who have nothing will be deprived of even the little they have." He then explained himself using a parable. "A man of importance was planning a business trip and called his employees into the office. He told them he needed them to look over his financial interests while he was out of town. To the first employee he gave a check for $20,000. To the second employee he gave a check for $8,000. And to a third employee he gave a check for $4,000. Each check was given in relation to the ability of the person who received it.

The man who had received $20,000 immediately went to work on his plan. Within a short time he had $40,000. The man who had been entrusted with $8,000 also doubled his money and now had $16,000. However, the third man hid his entire $4,000 in a pillow case and placed it at the bottom of his closet.

After a long absence, the boss returned to see how his investments were doing. He called the first man into his office, and the man reported, 'Sir, you entrusted me with $20,000 and I have turned it into $40,000.' 'Well done, my man!' said the boss. 'Because of your hard work I will make you a partner in the firm. You have shown that you can handle the responsibility.' The man who had been entrusted with $8000 also came and reported, 'I have doubled your money!' 'Well done! From now on I will trust you with even larger sums of money.'

But then, the man who had been given the smallest amount of money came forward. 'Sir,' he stuttered, 'You are an important man who takes whatever he wants and pushes people to their absolute limits. I was afraid of what you might do to me if I failed, so I hid your money in my closet. I didn't risk doing anything with it. Here is your $4000 back.' The boss angrily replied to him: 'You useless wimp! So you were afraid of me, were you? Then you should have done something with the money. At the very least, you could have put it in a savings account and earned a little interest. Take this fellow's money away and give it to the one with $40,000! Now get out of my sight!'[20]

Mark 12:1-8; 14:1-7; Luke 7:36-39

Jesus arrived in Bethany just outside of Jerusalem. He lodged in the house of Simon the leper and was sitting down to eat dinner. One of the women at the dinner presented Jesus with some very costly perfume which she poured over his head as a sign of her respect. Some of the other guests were angry at the woman's actions. They felt that the anointing of Jesus' head was a waste of money that could have been used for charitable purposes. The woman could feel the dirty looks from the other guests. But, knowing their thoughts, Jesus said, "Why are you holding a grudge against this woman? Her intentions were pure and she has done something truly good and honorable. For you will always have the poor with you and you can do good to them whenever you feel like it. However, I will not be here much longer."[21]

Later, in the evening, he shared this story with them: "A person owned a vineyard and rented it to some farmers so that they collect the crop for him. After a while he sent one of his slaves to the vineyard to collect the profits. But the farmers grabbed the slave, beat him almost to death and sent him back to the owner of the vineyard. The owner thought to himself, 'Perhaps these men made a mistake. Maybe they didn't realize that it was my slave.' So he sent another slave with an official seal. However, the farmers beat this slave as well. So the owner said to himself, 'I will send my son. Surely they will show respect for him.' But when the owner's son showed up at the vineyard, they grabbed him and beat him to death; knowing he was the rightful heir to the vineyard."

Remember What God has Wrought

Mark 14:22-24; I Corinthians 15

At about 6 p.m. on Thursday night, Jesus and his disciples gathered in a room to observe Passover. However, Jesus used the occasion to teach an important lesson on the Kingdom of

---

[20] Probably the most clearly Karmic of Jesus' parables.

[21] Similar to the Eastern concept of "Maya" – perhaps...

God. As he raised the bread to his lips, he looked at each disciple, one-by-one, and said, "This represents my body – as it will be broken for you." And then raising a glass, he said, "this represents my blood – shed for you. May this ceremony represent the truth of God's Kingdom. It is a breath away from consummation. Do this often to remember our essential unity, and the triumph of the Kingdom over even death. The Kingdom of the Living God is, in one word, 'Love.'"[22]

The Passion
Mark 14:43–15:37; Luke 22:52–53; John 18:2–12; I Corinthians 15:8

Late on Thursday night, nearing the midnight hour, Jesus and his Disciples camped at a place called "Gethsemane, " just outside of Jerusalem. Feeling sorrowful, Jesus walked into the woods to pray. He asked Peter, James, and John to come with him.

Having been led by one of Jesus' disciples, the police showed up where Jesus and his friends were gathered. The police seized Jesus and held him tightly. One of Jesus' disciples took out his sword to defend him, but Jesus ordered him to put it back. "Do you not know that all those who live by the sword, die by the sword?"[23]

Terrified, the rest of the disciples fled as fast as they could, leaving Jesus alone.[24] Eventually Jesus was brought before the High Priest – the religious authority of the Jewish Nation.[25]

The Priest had Jesus turned over to the secular ruler of the region, Pontius Pilate, who had Jesus flogged with a whip and then ordered his crucifixion.

Roman soldiers brought Jesus to a place called "Golgotha," which in English is translated "The Place of the Skull or 'Calvary.'" And Jesus was crucified there.

As he hung from the cross, in visible anguish, he recited Psalms for comfort as was the custom of the Jews. He could be

---
22 Many researchers omit the communion account as inauthentic; however it appears in every gospel and was well known by Paul. It is thus hard to explain how it became normative so early unless it went back to Jesus; at least in part.

23 another Karmic reference – both literally and metaphorically true

24 The gospels generally agree that Jesus was alone after his arrest. Thus it is unlikely that anyone would have had any first hand information about the details of his trial.

25 It is clear from the Torah that Jews were not to have such trials except in the "clear light of day"

heard quoting the 22nd Psalm, "My God, My God, why hast thou forsaken me? Why art thou so far from helping me, and from the words of my groaning?"[26]

There were some women observing from a distance among whom were Mary Magdalene, James mother — Mary, as well as the mother of James the Younger and Joses. Salome was also there.

These were the women that had been with him all along and assisted in his ministry and accompanied him to Jerusalem. As they looked upon Jesus' body they saw him take his last breath.

Mark 14:43–15:37; Luke 22:52–53; John 18:2-12; I Corinthians 15:8

Although it looked like the end, several days later,[27] Jesus appeared to Mary Magdalene,[28] the woman from whom he had driven out seven demons. For a time, Mary cherished the vision[29] in her heart.[30] Eventually, others in the Jerusalem community had Jesus experiences and discovered their common conviction.[31]

Later, Christ appeared to Peter and many others at a previously decided location in Galilee.[32]

The organized church began in Jerusalem and was headed by Jesus' brother, James, and Peter, as well as John Zebedee. In time, the group started by Mary Magdalene, and the group started by Peter joined forces and became indistinguishable.

Eventually, Paul of Tarsus also had a vision of the risen Jesus.[33]

---

26 In Aramaic, the 22nd Psalm begins "Eloi Eloi Lama Sabachthani."

27 Traditionally "three days." In some accounts it is "after three days," others "in three days." In fact, according to the chronology of the synoptics, there were only 1.6 days between Jesus' crucifixion and resurrection. "Three days" is probably an idiomatic phrase meaning "after a while."

28 Mary Magdalene appears first in every list of "women." She is in every resurrection account and the Gospel of John clearly makes her the first witness to the resurrection. This is difficult to explain in the male-dominated culture of the 1st Century... unless it actually happened...

29 The earliest resurrection account is from Paul. He doesn't seem to be describing a physical appearance. Also see note #31

30 The original ending of Mark says that Mary was in shock, and told no one. The parallel account in Luke says she left the tomb joyfully and ran to tell the apostles.

31 The oldest sources do not contain clear resurrection narratives. The earliest documentable source of information is the words of Paul and he seems to interpret Jesus' resurrection in a spiritual rather than a literally physical sense. His words on the subject were composed before any of the gospels. See I Corinthians 15, particularly vs. 5-8. Also see John 20:14-17

32 *cf* Matthew 26:32; 28:7: This was likely some time later, if for no other reason than Galilee was an 8-day walk from Jerusalem

33 See Appendix I for a more robust speculation on what happened after Jesus' death.

Chapter 3

Conclusions

I have reserved this, the final portion of the book, to divulge my personal reflections on the theology of Jesus. Although I believe in good conscience that my opinions follow from the evidence, they are nevertheless my personal opinions and should be considered as separate from the more rigorous and factual approach of the earlier chapters of this book. Since I have already made it clear that this section is set aside for my personal reflections, I have dispensed with repeating "in my opinion," as well as avoidance of personal pronouns.

Who was Jesus? In the briefest possible terms, Jesus was a high consciousness mystic – perhaps the highest level mystic that has yet been born. A "mystic" is a person who cultivates a direct experience of the transcendent (*i.e.* "God") – and in Jesus' case, shares the insights with others. I believe this is, in fact, what Jesus meant by "prayer." Prayer, to Jesus, is a state of firm intention and meditation to seek the fire of God within one's self. To perfect this state (*i.e.* "pray without ceasing"[1]) is to live in the "Kingdom of God" – where one's actions come from the spiritual self, and not from the carnal, selfish, physical self.

Clearly, Jesus was also a man of great compassion-in-action; however, this compassion was a natural by-product of his close

---
1 Not a direct quote from Jesus but representative of his thought – *cf* I Thessalonians 5:17

relationship with God rather than an end in itself. Living fully and completely in the Kingdom of God, one can do no other than to practice compassion to one's fellow man in thought, deed, and action. Jesus showed us the way, and did not compromise with the world.[2]

Jesus had much in common with other Eastern mystics[3] across history, both in message and behavior. His essential message was to consciously grow close to God (*i.e.* "The Kingdom of God"), and in so doing, take responsibility for one's spiritual evolution and intentions. A soul's progress along this path could be measured, according to Jesus, by the capacity one has to love one's fellow human being.[4]

Although it is certainly not explicit in his words, I suspect that the Historical Jesus believed in some sort of reincarnation[5] as well. This is clearly speculation on my part, but in addition to being concordant with the message of virtually all other mystics, there seems to also be some circumstantial evidence in Jesus' own words. For example, in John 9:

> *And his disciples asked him, saying, Rabbi, who sinned; this man, or his parents, that he was born blind? Jesus answered, Neither this man nor his parents sinned. It was only that the works of God might be displayed upon him.*

When would the man have sinned? It would have had to have been either in the womb, which seems unlikely, or before he was born. Jesus takes the statement at face value and does not correct the questioner. There are also many parables about gradual growth which are consistent with a long-term process of perfection into the Kingdom. Practically every high-level mystic, regardless of background or religion, has professed belief in some type of reincarnation.[6] This includes many Western Christian mystics, both Protestant and Catholic.[7]

---

[2] See suggested meaning of "martyr" in Chapter 1

[3] Americans tend to associate mystics with the Eastern world, but there have also been many Catholic Mystics in the West such as Thomas Kempis and Francis of Assisi

[4] *cf* John 13:34-35

[5] This is a term with a lot of baggage. I don't necessarily mean all of the implications of Hindu theology here, but rather a recycling of energy – a recycling of one's essential authentic self over many lifetimes, for the purpose of growth in consciousness.

Conclusions 49

In sum, there are two themes in Jesus' teaching that are stressed more than any other: 1) The Kingdom of God, described previously, and 2) Karma. The term "Karma" may be unfamiliar to many Westerners, and the term itself is not used by Jesus. However, the concept of Karma is on almost every page of the book of Mark. Karma is the cosmic principle of cause and effect: The idea that all actions, whether good or evil, must run their natural course. All actions involving others must also be experienced by the doer. Thus, the only way to improve one's situation is to modify the way one acts and chooses. We are thus completely responsible for our outcomes and states. This is the universal Law of Karma.[8] Jesus often ended a healing with the words "Now, go, and sin no more," illustrating the role of choice and action in Salvation.

Another peculiarity in the ethos of the historical Jesus relative to mainstream tradition is his occasional seeming disinterest in the unfairness of the world. In fact, at times he can be seen validating inequality and suffering as normative. This is best reflected in statements such as "the poor you will always have among you,"[9] "the rain falls on the just and on the unjust,"[10] and the Parable of the Tares.[11]

From a Western world-view perspective this is puzzling and seems to contradict Jesus' compassionate nature. However, from an Eastern mindset, it makes sense. What I am getting at here is the concept of "Maya"[12] in many Eastern religions. It is a metaphysical and ontological statement about what is real. Maya implies that the world is fundamentally unfair on

---

6 cf Wisdom 8:19-20, in the Christian Apocrypha, for example

7 The "church father," Origen, espoused a theory of the pre-existence of souls similar in many ways to reincarnation. He wrote in the period 150 years after the death of Jesus.

8 A common simple definition is: There is no difference, ultimately, between causes and effects.

9 Mark 14:7

10 Matthew 5:45

11 Matthew 13:24-30; also known as "Parable of Wheat and Tares," or "Parable of the Weeds."

12 I am using this Hindu term as shorthand. There are many ways to reference this principle from many diverse cultures and languages. It is also contained somewhat in *Karma Yoga* and to some degree *Karma Sakata Sammaditthi* and *Amoha* in Buddhism, for example.

purpose.[13] This stands in stark relief to the Western idea that the world can and must be "fixed."

Often, Westerners assume that the purpose of religion (and by extension the purpose of Jesus' teaching) is to fix the problems of the world. For example, money should be given to a poor person as a first step to curing their poverty – thus the motive to action is change. However, from a "Maya" perspective, the motivation to action is compassion, not change. One gives to the poor person because of what it does to the giver, as well as what it does to the receiver. In other words, the concept of Maya is closely linked into the concept of Karma discussed previously. Both point towards growth as the currency of the universe.

I believe this is what Jesus meant in these enigmatic statements where he seems to deviate from his compassionate mission. And, it seems likely that he would look at things this way given his culture and level of spiritual insight.

Obviously the Jesus described in this chapter differs greatly from commonly-held (particularly "fundamentalist") conceptions of Jesus. However, I do not believe that Jesus ever claimed to be a "sacrifice for sin" (Atonement) in any juridical, literal sense of the terms. As discussed in Chapter 1, this Atonement Theology is largely absent in the synoptic gospels, and is completely absent in the most ancient Gospel, the Gospel of Mark. The Jesus of the book of Mark, even before being subject to critical analysis and alteration, is strikingly similar to the words and message of other mystical sages throughout human history. Jesus' message of Karma, Relationship-with-God[14], Compassion-Towards-Others, and the dichotomy of the Spiritual Man vs. the Carnal Man is almost indistinguishable from the core message of Buddha and Krishna, for example.[15]

So, is there any "Good News" here? The Good News is you can't loose. Every honest and sincere "good thing" you have

---

[13] The literal meaning of Maya is 'illusion,' so my argument here is an implication of that broad principle

[14] An Eastern mystic probably wouldn't use the term "God" as it evokes the idea of a personal human-like being, but here I am assuming that the underlying idea is essentially the same.

[15] Gandhi may be a decent modern example

Conclusions 51

ever done has had a positive impact on your development.[16] You are evolving upward and out of the carnal, and into the Spirit. That is the Law.[17] There is more good news. God is not "up in the sky." He is as close as your heart. While everyone is in this process of growing, the speed of growth and its resultant effects on contentment are under our control: The fastest and most reliable way to find God is to look within and intentionally make the Search-for-God highest priority.[18]

Although the game of life is "rigged" to facilitate your (and everyone else's) spiritual development,[19] it is possible to accelerate one's path to enlightenment and growth in consciousness. According to Jesus this is done by (in order of Jesus' emphasis); 1) Consciously deciding to put the quest for God first in one's life,[20] 2) Consistently living from one's Spirit instead of Carnal desires,[21] 3) By practicing (literally) compassion towards others,[22] and 4) non-attachment to physical things.[23] This is "Salvation"[24] as taught by the Historical Jesus.

---

16 ...of consciousness or level-of-consciousness

17 ...of Karma

18 *cf* The Greatest Commandment

19 ...including experiencing 'suffering' which can be a great tool for character growth, unpleasant as it is in the short run

20 Mark 12:29-30

21 Matthew 6:19-21; Mark 8:32-33

22 Mark 1:41; Mark 14:6

23 Mark 8:34-37; Luke 17:33

24 or, perhaps, the "process of Salvation"

Appendices

Appendix I

What Happened to Jesus' Body?

A suggestion of how Mark may have originally ended based upon the words of Paul and historical speculation.

The book of Mark ends abruptly at verse eight (16:8) with the following, "The women then getting out, fled from the tomb, seized with trembling and consternation; but said nothing to any one, they were so terrified." What follows is a much later-written ending that seems to have been composed through a mild re-working of the original ending of Matthew, which was written much later. Since Paul never talks about the details of Jesus' death and resurrection, and since the ending of Mark is missing, the earliest detailed account we have of these events is 60 years after the fact. This is a staggering amount of time in the ancient world with a 95% illiteracy rate, an average life expectancy of less than 30 years, and no modern media to accurately store and transfer ideas. Thus by looking at circumstantial evidence and reading between the lines of Paul's letters, I have come up with a proposed account of what might have actually occurred after verse eight in Mark.

The women then getting out, fled from the tomb, seized with trembling and consternation; but said nothing to any one, they were so terrified, then.....

1. Jesus' followers convince a wealthy Jew to negotiate with the Romans for Jesus' body. He gets tacit approval from the Roman authorities, but the body never arrives at the tomb. This explains the Joseph of Aramathea legend and why there are so many conflicting stories about the tomb. Paul never mentions the empty tomb or Joseph of Aramathea and he wrote before any of the gospels were composed (Mark 15:43; John 19:38–39).

2. Meanwhile, Jesus' apostles return to Galilee following Jesus' prior instructions (Mark 16:7).

3. Locally, in Jerusalem, Mary Magdalene has a mystical experience of Jesus. She is reticent at first but eventually shares her visions with others. She discovers that other local followers of Jesus have had similar experiences.

4. Meanwhile in Galilee, the apostles have a mass mystical experience of the risen Jesus (I Corinthians 15:4-5). They see this as a final cosmic proof that man can survive death and be with God forever (I Corinthians 15:20, 22, 45, 48, 57). Then they make their way back to Jerusalem to start the Church within Judaism. James was first leader of the church (Acts 12:17, 21:17–18; I Corinthians 15:7; Galatians 2:11–12). At some point their group discovers the Mary Magdalene group and they join forces.

5. Paul of Tarsus, a Jewish persecutor of Christians, eventually is converted to the growing Mystic/Atonement sect of Christianity (see Appendix 3). At first he met with limited success and returned to his home at Tarsus. About nine years later, while meditating there, Paul has a full-blown mystical experience where he believes that he is "caught up to heaven" and receives instructions from God himself (II Corinthians 12:2–4). He begins his base-of-operations for a ministry to the Gentiles from Antioch. (Acts 9; 13–14; Galatians 1). [*c.* 43 A.D.]

6. By about 50 A.D., four sects of Christianity are becoming distinct; the Karmic; the Mystic; the Eschatological; and the Atonement sect (see Appendix 3).

7. The death of Judaism within the Roman empire and the resistance of the Jews to writing led to the eventual extinction of all but the Atonement and to a lesser extent the Mystic strains by about 70 A.D. Furthermore, the character of the thinking rapidly becomes more distinctly Greek and less distinctly Jewish, the process culminating in Nicaea, 325 A.D.

Appendix II

A summary (digression *re:*) what Paul says the church "always" believed.

As the gospels were written *c.* 70–100 A.D., these words from Paul are our earliest written account of Christian theology and Jesus' life (I Corinthians 15, *c.* 56 A.D.. Here is a summary of what Paul said, paraphrased for the modern context:

1. **Christ conquered death ("Died for our sins")**

    "Sin" in Paul's culture was an explanation of why men had to die (animal-like) deaths. It was believed that this was due to God's holiness. Thus one had to be sinless to continue consciousness after death. Thus "sin" = "imperfection / shortcoming / other-ness."

2. **Christ was buried**

3. **Christ proved his victory over death by communicating after death to his disciples**

    In the context of I Corinthians 15, Paul seems to be arguing that Jesus provided proof that man can survive death – a principle denied by many Jews of his day who asserted that death was the end.

4. **The mystical experiences of Christ were widespread for a time**

Paul implies that the appearances of Jesus were mystical ("spiritual bodies") rather than literal and physical as presented in Gospels of Matthew, Luke, and John.

Appendix III

Proposed early divisions within Christianity: Atonement, Mystical, Eschatological, and Karmic.

In its earliest formative period Christianity was theologically diverse. It was centered around an experience of Jesus, but the explanation of that experience took many forms. The following essay attempts to chart these early differences as an explanation of seeming contradictions in the New Testament which was written over a 50-year period and is not chronologically ordered in its canonical form.

Almost immediately following Jesus' death there were many different interpretations of his life and message. For a time, the original disciples struggled to understand what had happened. Gradually these differences coalesced into four different streams compounded by geographic and cultural differences. After the fall of Judaism in the Roman Empire and the influx of Greek culture and language, only two of the original strains survived, and of those two, one in particular has characterized Christianity since the 300's A.D.:

The surviving strain is the **"Atonement"** sect. This strain is most like modern organized Christianity and stresses the substitutionary death of Jesus as a sacrifice for sin above all else. This strain was popularized by Paul and the Greeks, although Paul's emphasis on the Atonement pales in comparison of that of many modern "mainstream" Christian movements such as the Roman Catholic Church and the Southern Baptist Convention. This theological orientation can be seen most strongly in the late-written (perhaps 100 A.D.) Book of Hebrews in the New Testament. The Gospels of Luke and John also show an Atonement emphasis.

The second surviving, but less emphasized in the modern world, is the "**Mystical**" sect. This group was best represented in ancient times by the Gnostics and to a lesser degree, the group that produced the Gospel of John. The Mystical sect saw the Jesus-experience as primarily a direct experience with the sacred. They emphasized knowing the living Jesus and had little interest in historical matters and Jesus' earthly biography. My thesis is that Paul was originally recruited by this sect, but also had one foot in the Atonement sect. Paul always talks about the "living Christ" and never mentions Jesus' earthly deeds.

The third sect of early Christianity was the "**Eschatological**" sect. This group was expecting an imminent end to the physical world and an establishment of a literal Kingdom of God on Earth. This group died out for pretty obvious reasons—the end did not come. However, a careful reading of Paul's letters shows that the earlier the letter was written, the more concern there was with Jesus' quick return. Thus, this was still a viable orientation in Paul's time. There are also several "end of the world" vignettes in the Gospels.

The fourth sect, and the one most closely related to the Historical Jesus' ethos, in the opinion of the current author, is the "**Karmic**" sect. The Karmic sect was thoroughly Jewish (as was Jesus himself) and essentially died when Judaism "died" within the Roman Empire. The Karmic sect stressed personal responsibility before God and a slow spiritual evolution. The ideology of the Karmic sect is best represented by the book of James, as well as the Gospel of Mark. The connection with James is pretty obvious as James was quite likely the father of the organized Christian church. Although it is doubtful that James himself contributed to the eponymous canonical book, it is assumed that his name became associated with it because it shared the basic ideas of his sect. Mark preserves the Karmic ideology because it preserves the most ancient sayings of the Historical Jesus as discussed in the earlier chapters of the present project.

Appendix IV

Chronological Summary of Important Contradictions and Errors in the Canonical Gospels in the Same Order as the Gospel of Mark, Beginning in Chapter I

The following abbreviated list of errors is intended to cast doubt on the strict and rigid "fundamentalist" interpretive system of understanding the New Testament. It is not intended to cast doubt on the basic thrust of the New Testament and is assumed to not be threatening to those with more interpretive views. Fundamentalists generally claim that every word of the bible is literally accurate. When pressed they sometimes assert that if one word of the bible is not true, that the entire Faith falls apart. This section exposes the inanity of such a position. Clearly the ideas in the New Testament developed over time and were filtered through the individual psyches of its authors.

1. Jesus is only referred to as the "one and only" Son in the Gospel of John. He is never referred to as such in the synoptic gospels. (Mark 1:1; John 1:18)

2. There are many inconsistencies and differences in the Genealogies of Jesus which cannot be reconciled except through the most tortuous misuse of logic and deduction. (Matthew 1:2–17; Luke 3:23–38)

3. There are problems with Luke's dating of Jesus' birth and childhood.

   a. Quirinius could not have been governor at the time of Jesus birth, according to several objective historical sources. He was a leader in that area in the year 6 A.D.; at least nine years after Jesus' birth (Luke 2:1–2).

   b. Quirinius was never "governor;" he was only a legate.

   c. Palestine was not under Syrian control at the time anyway, and even if Quirinius had been governor, he would not have had jurisdiction. Palestine would have been Herod's jurisdiction.

   d. There is no record, outside of the Bible, that Rome ever took a "worldwide" census. All Roman censuses were local. And even local Roman censuses were only required of Roman citizens – not foreigners living within the borders.

4. There are no miraculous birth stories either in the Gospel of John or the Gospel of Mark; nor are they ever mentioned by Paul. Mark implies that Jesus was born and raised in Nazareth (Mark 1:9; Mark 6:1,4). John may have also made this assumption (*cf* Mark 6:1 & John 7:41–43).

5. Luke dates the beginning of John the Baptist's ministry with the leadership of Lysanias. Luke is wrong about the tenure of Lysanias (Luke 3:1). In fact, Lysanias died in 36 B.C. – at least 60 years before John the Baptist started his ministry.

6. In the very next sentence (Luke 3:2), Luke says that Caiaphas and Annas shared the high priesthood. In fact, Caiaphas was the only high priest, according to recorded history.

7. There are inconsistencies in the way the Holy Spirit is said to have rested on Jesus at his baptism. In Mark and Matthew, only Jesus "sees" the dove and hears the voice of God. In Luke and John (written later), it is described as a public experience in which everyone present saw the dove

and heard the voice (Mark 1:10–12; Matthew 3: 16–18; Luke 3:21–23; John 1: 32–35).

8. This one is relatively minor, but worth pointing out, I think. Jesus is reported as going "40 days" without food in his temptation in the wilderness (Mark 1:12–13; Matthew 4:2; Luke 4:2). This would be the extreme outside edge of survivability. Very few people, particularly those without a lot of excess adipose tissue, would survive beyond 30 days. In the modern era, Gandhi, who was probably much closer to Jesus' size than a typical modern Western man, almost died after a 21-day fast. Also, Gandhi was not "in the wilderness" and regularly drank fluids during his fast.

9. When Mark has Jesus quoting the Old Testament, he quotes it inaccurately. As Jesus tells the story of King David eating the Showbread, he says "Did you never read what David and his attendants did, in a strait, when they were hungry, how he entered the tabernacle of God, in the days of Abiathar the high priest, and eat the loaves of the presence?" However, Abiathar was not the high priest. The high priest that year was Ahimelech (I Samuel, Chapter 21).

10. In the story of the sinful-woman-who-anointed-Jesus (identified as Mary, sister of Lazarus in the Gospel of John account), Luke disagrees with Mark on how Jesus was anointed. Mark says that the woman anointed his head, Luke says that she anointed his feet (*cf* Mark 14:3; Luke 7:37–38). Mark's account is older and it could be that Luke was uncomfortable with the image of a woman anointing Jesus' head, which would put her in a position of equality with Jesus, and with males in general.

11. Mark makes a major geographical error in 7:31. Sidon is not on the way to Tyre; it is north of Tyre.

12. There are discrepancies regarding how long Jesus was "in the tomb." Mark (9:31) says that Jesus will rise "after three days;" Matthew (17:23) says "on the third day." In fact neither of these matches the actual chronology described at the end of the Gospels. According to all four, Jesus was "in

Appendix IV 63

the tomb" for 1.6 days. Some scholars have suggested that "three days" is actually an idiomatic phrase which means something like "after a while."

13. The synoptic Gospels put the "cleansing of the temple" at the end of Jesus' ministry as the catalyzing event leading to his death. John has the event nearer to the beginning of Jesus' ministry (*cf* Mark 11:15–16 & John 2:13–15).

14. In the synoptics, Jesus institutes Communion in the context of Passover and on the day of Passover. John has it happen a day before Passover without a connection to the Passover meal (*cf* Mark 14:12 & John 13:1).

15. There are conflicting accounts as to what happened to Judas. Matthew (27:5) say Judas was overcome with guilt and hanged himself. Acts 1:18 says that Judas fell and his insides "burst open." The Acts account goes on to say that Judas himself had purchased a field. In the Matthew account, the chief priests bought the field. And finally, the prophecy that was supposedly fulfilled, is quoted in Matthew (27:9) as having come from Jeremiah. In fact the quoted prophecy comes from Zechariah 11:12–13, not Jeremiah.

16. According to John's account (19:14), Jesus was crucified at noon ("the sixth hour"). However, according to Mark, he was crucified at 9 a.m. ("the third hour").

17. According to John, Jesus carried his own cross (19:17). In Mark and the synoptics, Simon of Cyrene was forced to carry the cross for Jesus (*cf* Mark 15:21).

18. Luke says that "two men" were standing in Jesus' tomb (24:4). Mark says only one man (16:5), and Matthew describes one angel instead of a mere man (28:2–3).

19. There are differences in the accounts of who saw the empty tomb first. Mark 16:1, describes a party of three: Mary Magdalene, Mary-mother-of-James, and Salome. Matthew describes a party of two; only the two Marys went to the tomb (28:1). Luke says "women" but does not specify a number. John has Mary discovering the tomb all by herself

(20:1). Curiously, the Apostle Paul, who was writing before any of the gospels were written, says nothing about the women and claims that Peter was the first to come to the knowledge of the risen Lord (I Corinthians 15:5).

20. The last original verse in the book of Mark is 16:8. In this verse, the women are described as being in shock when they found the tomb empty and that they told no one what they saw. This conflicts directly with the accounts in the other gospels. The parallel account in Matthew (28:7–8) says very nearly the opposite: The women are described as being "joyful" instead of afraid and then are said to have gone immediately to tell the disciples what they saw. The accounts in Luke and John are similar (Luke 24:9; John 20:18).

21. The Gospels disagree sharply on how long the risen (physical) Jesus stayed around before his assumption into heaven. The Luke account (24:50–51) assumes a more-or-less immediate assumption. In Acts, it is clearly stated that Jesus stayed around 40 days after his resurrection (1:3). The book of John implies that it was eight days (20:26). The apostle Paul, writing in I Corinthians 15 seems to imply a non-physical resurrection and recons himself as the last direct experiencer of Jesus (or at least the last experiencer to have a vision of the same quality as the apostles). This would mean that Jesus' appearances continued for three to twelve years, depending upon how one interprets the Pauline life-chronology (see Appendix I).

Bibliography/Sources

American Standard Version of the Holy Bible (1901). Public domain.

Armstrong, K.A. (1993). *A History of God: The 4,000-Year Quest of Judaism, Christianity, and Islam.* Ballantine Books, New York.

Armstrong, K.A. (2007). *The Bible: A Biography.* Grove Press, New York.

Bercot, David W. (2003). *The Kingdom that Turned the World Upside Down.* Scroll Publishing, Amberson, PA.

Bloom, Harold (1992). *The American Religion.* Simon & Schuster, New York.

Book of Confessions: Study Edition (1996). Geneva Press, Louisville, KY.

Borg, M. (1995). *Meeting Jesus Again for the First Time: The Historical Jesus and the Heart of Contemporary Faith.* Harper One, New York.

Burkett, Delbert (1999). *The Son of Man Debate: A History and Evaluation.* Cambridge University Press. New York.

Campbell, Alexander (1835). *The Christian System.* Gospel Advocate Restoration Reprints, Nashville.

Campbell, Alexander (1832). *The Living Oracles, 3rd Edition.* [New Testament in Modern English from the Critical Greek Text]. Gospel Advocate Restoration Reprints, Nashville.

Carse, J.P. (1997). *The Gospel of the Beloved Disciple.* Harper, San Francisco.

The Complete Bible: An American Translation (1951). Edgar J. Goodspeed (Ed.). The University of Chicago Press.

Crossan, John D. (1992). *The Historical Jesus: The Life of a Mediterranean Jewish Peasant.* Harper, San Francisco.

Danzier, Davis D. (1998). *Betrayal of Jesus: Twenty-First Century Challenges for Christians.* Word Wizards Publications, Escondido, CA.

Ehrman, B.D. (2007). *Misquoting Jesus: The Story Behind Who Changed the Bible and Why.* Harper One, New York.

Ehrman, B.D. (2003). *Lost Christianities: The Battles for Scripture and the Faiths We Never Knew.* Oxford.

Fisk, William Lyons (1995). *The Scottish High Church Tradition in America: An Essay in Scotch-Irish Ethnoreligious History.* University Press in America, Lanham, MD.

Funk, Robert W. (1999). *The Gospel of Jesus: According to the Jesus Seminar.* Polebridge Press, Santa Rosa, CA.

Girzone, Joseph F. (2000). *Jesus, His Life and Teachings.* Image Books, New York, NY.

Goodspeed, E.J. (1956). *A Life of Jesus.* Harper Torchlight, New York.

Holman, John (2008). *The Return of the Perennial Philosophy: The Supreme Vision of Western Esotericism.* Watkins Publishing, London.

Henson, John (2005). *Good as New: A Radical Retelling of the Scriptures.* O Books, Great Britain.

Hoover, R. W. (2010). *Was Jesus' Resurrection an Historical Event?* The Fourth R, Vol. 23. No. 5, 5-12.

Hughes, Richard T. (1995). *Reclaiming a Heritage.* Restoration Quarterly, Vol. 37 No. 3.

Interpreters Bible (1951). Nolan B. Harmon (Ed.). Abingdon Press, New York.

The King James Bible (1611). Public domain in the United States of America.

Keating, Thomas (2006). *Open Mind, Open Heart: 20th Anniversary Edition.* Continuum Books, New York.

Kinnaman, D., & Lyons, G. (2007). *Un-Christian: What a New Generation Really Thinks About Christianity and Why it Matters.* Baker Books, Grand Rapids, MI.

Jefferson, Thomas (1820). *The Life and Morals of Jesus of Nazareth.* [various publishers].
Kirk, C. T. (2010). *The Holy Catechism of Yeshua Barnasha.* Lucas Park Books, St. Louis.
Marion, Jim (2004). *Death of the Mythic God: The Rise of Evolutionary Spirituality.* Hampton Roads Publishing, Charlottesville, VA.
Marion, Jim (2000). *Putting on the Mind of Christ.* Hampton Roads Publishing, Charlottesville, VA.
McDowell, Josh (1999). *The New Evidence that Demands a Verdict.* Thomas Nelson Publishing, Nashville.
McKenzie, J.L. (1965). *Dictionary of the Bible.* Macmillan, New York.
McLaren, B.D. (2006). *A Generous Orthodoxy.* Zondervan, Grand Rapids, MI.
McLaren, B.D. (2011). *A New Kind of Christianity: Ten Questions that are Transforming the Faith.* HarperOne, New York.
McKnight, Scot (2010). *Jesus vs. Paul.* Christianity Today, Vol. 54, No. 12, 24-29.
Meyer, Marvin (2005). *The Unknown Sayings of Jesus.* New Seeds Publishing, Boston.
Myers, D.G. (1992). *The Pursuit of Happiness: Discovering the Pathway to Fulfillment, Well-Being, and Enduring Personal Joy.* Quill Publishing, New York, NY.
New Analytical Bible and Dictionary of the Bible. (1973). Dickson, J.A. (Ed.). World Bible Publishers, Iowa Falls, IA.
The New Testament from Twenty-Six Translations. (1967). Vaughan, Curtis (Ed.). Zondervan, Grand Rapids, MI.
NIV Study Bible. (2002). Barker, K.L. & Burdick (Eds.). Zondervan, Grand Rapids, MI.
The Oxford Dictionary of the Christian Church, Third Edition. (2005). Cross, F.L., & Livingstone, E.A. (Eds.). Oxford University Press, USA.
Packer, J.I., Merrill, C.T., & White, W.W. (1982). *The World of the New Testament.* Thomas Nelson, Nashville.
Pelikan, Jaroslav (1985). *Jesus Through the Centuries: His Place in the History of Culture.* Harper & Row, New York.

Piatt, Christian (2011). *Banned Questions about Jesus.* Chalice Press, St. Louis, MO.

Ray, Jack L. (2010). *Faith, Opinion and Charity: Defining Campbell's Maxim.* In Neil W. Anderson (Ed.), Gospel Advocate (pp. 21-23). Nashville.

Reimarus, Herman Samuel (1768). *Fragments.* [various publishers].

Sanders, E.P. (1977). *Paul and Palestinian Judaism: A Comparison of Patterns of Religion.* Fortress Press, Philadelphia.

Servetus, Michael (1553). *Christianismi Restitutio.* [various publishers].

Shanks, Hershel (1993). *An Unpublished Dead Sea Scroll Text Parallels Luke's Infancy Narrative.* In H. Shanks (Ed.), *Understanding the Dead Sea Scrolls* (pp. 203-204). New York: Vintage Books.

Spong, John Shelby (1991). *Rescuing the Bible from Fundamentalism: A Bishop Rethinks the Meaning of Scripture.* Harper, San Francisco.

Spong, John Shelby (2007). *Jesus for the Non-religious.* Harper, New York.

The Twentieth Century New Testament: A Translation into Modern English Made From the Original Greek by a Company of Twenty from all Sections of the Christian Church (1904). Higgs, M.K., & Malan, E.M. (Eds.). Fleming H. Revell Company, New York.

Synopsis of the Four Gospels (1993). Kurt Aland (Ed.). German Bible Society, Stuttgart.

Vanderkam, James C. (1993). *The Dead Sea Scrolls and Christianity.* In H. Shanks (Ed.), *Understanding the Dead Sea Scrolls* (pp. 181-202). New York: Vintage Books.

Vermes, Geza (1983). *Jesus and the World of Judaism.* Fortress Press. Minneapolis.

Vine's Expository Dictionary of New Testament Words. (1952). Vine, W. E. (Ed.). Marshall Pickering Communications Publishing and Barbour Books. Uhrichsville, OH.

Wilson, Ian (1984). *Jesus: The Evidence.* Harper, San Francisco, CA.

Wright, N.T. (1999). *The Challenge of Jesus: Rediscovering Who Jesus Was and Is.* IVP Academic Press, Downers Grove, Il.

Yadin, Yigael (1993). *The Temple Scroll.* In H. Shanks (Ed.), *Understanding the Dead Sea Scrolls* (pp. 87-112). New York: Vintage Books.

Yogananda, P. (2007). *The Yoga of Jesus.* Self-Realization Fellowship Publishing, Los Angeles.

www.ingramcontent.com/pod-product-compliance
Lightning Source LLC
Chambersburg PA
CBHW071632040426
42452CB00009B/1591